Dr. Matthew Stevens[...] writing and communication are timely, prophetic, [...] articulate. In *Abba* he points you to the identity of God in order to reveal your authentic identity. This teaching provides much-needed answers to some of life's biggest questions. Abba will set you free from many lies and traps of the enemy and set you on course to be the world changer that you are called to be!

—RYAN LeSTRANGE
FOUNDER, TRIBE NETWORK/
RYAN LeSTRANGE MINISTRIES
AUTHOR, *OVERCOMING SPIRITUAL ATTACK*

At a time when the world—and even many in the church—are confused about who they really are, Matthew Stevenson offers compassionate guidance to people who have suffered father hurts, deal with rejection issues, and struggle to truly understand God's heart in *Abba*. With keen insight and a relatable style Matthew sets the stage for readers to receive a revelation of God's love that brings healing to known and hidden wounds in their souls. I highly recommend this book.

—JENNIFER LeCLAIRE
SENIOR EDITOR, *CHARISMA* MAGAZINE
DIRECTOR, AWAKENING HOUSE OF PRAYER
AUTHOR, *JEZEBEL'S PUPPETS*

Abba deals with the important subject of identity. A revelation of the Father is essential in walking in purpose and destiny. Dr. Matthew Stevenson challenges the misconceptions of the Father and challenges us to walk in the truth of who He is. This book will provoke you and help you adjust your thinking. Dr. Stevenson is always stretching his audience to think outside of the box of religion and tradition. The truth sets us free. Let the truths of this book set you free from any limitations of your understanding of God. I pray the Lord will give you understanding as you consider what is said and taught. Walk in your purpose and identity, and fulfill the plan of God for your life.

—APOSTLE JOHN ECKHARDT
OVERSEER, CRUSADERS CHURCH
BEST-SELLING AUTHOR

ABBA

ABBA

MATTHEW L. STEVENSON III

CHARISMA
HOUSE

Cover design by Justin Evans

Visit the author's website at matthewstevensonworldwide.com and experiencegodasfather.com.

Library of Congress Cataloging-in-Publication Data:
An application to register this book for cataloging has been submitted to the Library of Congress.
International Standard Book Number: 978-1-62999-181-8
E-book ISBN: 978-1-62999-182-5

While the author has made every effort to provide accurate Internet addresses at the time of publication, neither the publisher nor the author assumes any responsibility for errors or for changes that occur after publication.

17 18 19 20 21 — 9 8 7 6 5 4 3 2 1
Printed in the United States of America

To my children,
Micah, Naila, and Karis,
along with my amazing wife,
Kamilah

CONTENTS

INTRODUCTION

That I may know him, and the power of his resurrection, and the fellowship of his sufferings, being made conformable unto his death.

∞∞∞ PHILIPPIANS 3:10 ∞∞∞

OUR WORLD IS in the midst of an identity crisis. This crisis is driven by immigration, globalization, nationalism, humanism, and fear of the future, and it affects not only national governments and economies but also the church. The identity crisis we see today is the fruit of what began when ordinary men and women rose to positions of power and influence before they came to know and master their identity. It is a dangerous thing to have great influence and an unsettled identity. Unresolved identity has produced uncertainty, fear, and a population of people who are ruled by the passions of their own wisdom and sin nature. God's design is that we would first have a clear understanding of our identity as sons and daughters.

On the earth, second to the Word of God and the Holy Ghost, your identity is the most important thing you have. Your identity dictates your actions, responses, thoughts, leadership abilities, and ultimately everything you do and say in your lifetime. If I were to interview you about the hardest part of your life, the pain points in your story, all roads would likely lead to a concerted assault on your identity. Now, this assault may have come through different means, tools, and resources, but no matter the means of assault Satan's goal is the same—to find any opportunity to distort how you see yourself. Satan knows that if he can get you to adopt an inaccurate or partial view of your identity, you will eventually take this identity crisis into your family life, career, church, or ministry. He wants to lead you into a war with the purposes of God for your life. So you cannot look to personality and spiritual gift tests to show you your identity. These quizzes have legitimacy, but they give an incomplete picture of who you are. Who you are, what you are able to do, and what you currently possess in gifts and talents are not the complete story of who God created you to be. God's identity for your life is bigger and broader, and it far outweighs your talents and abilities.

I frequently counsel people on who God has called them to be, or which office in the fivefold ministry they should actively pursue. The responses I receive to this counseling vary from relief to confusion. Those who are relieved are affirmed in their understanding of who they thought themselves to be. Those who are confused are heartbroken because sadly they built their lives around labels, titles, talents, and abilities. The revelation of who they really are is not met with a great deal of excitement. They are disappointed because they have used titles and their talents to try to bring meaning to their lives. They hid behind these titles because they didn't know who they were; they could not figure out their identity. They had not reconciled with God their true identity. I have often seen people who have experienced wounds, hurts, or trauma in life resort to self-protective behaviors, including masking themselves with titles and labels. They also gravitate toward the environments and supports that they think bring meaning and value to the wounded and undefined parts of their identity. However, when those structures are shaken, these individuals find themselves in deadly cycles and crises because they never dealt with the brokenness that impacted their identity formation.

Every human being needs to have his or her identity proved and secured before entering greater levels of responsibility. The only way to have a proven and secure identity is to see the identity of God. This is why Paul said in Philippians 3:10 that his goal was to "know [God], and the power of his resurrection, and the fellowship of his sufferings, being made conformable unto his death." Paul realized that his identity was inherently connected to the identity of God. If he could know more about God's identity, understand the power of Christ's resurrection, partner with the Holy Spirit to crucify his sin nature, and live by the Spirit of God, then Paul knew his life would be secure.

The mandate to know God was not just for Paul; it is for every human being. Yet the majority of us are not aware that God has an identity. We do not understand that God has tastes—there are things He likes and things He dislikes. God has things to say about Himself. God has an identity, and He desires to show it to us, for in His identity we will find our own. It is critical that we understand God as He truly is and not as we have made Him to be in our own eyes.

Too many people feel they understand God because of a few brief encounters with Him. This is akin to seeing someone in a small group or a crowd for just a few moments or maybe overhearing him sharing a point about himself, such as his favorite coffee or the most recent movie he has seen. However, those few interactions and bits of knowledge do not mean you know this person, and they do not grant you the right to claim intimate knowledge of that person. They certainly do not permit you to represent that individual's thoughts, moods, or intentions to others. Unfortunately this has been the approach the church and society have taken in communicating God's identity. We have not spent enough time getting to know God, yet we speak on His behalf every single day with our lives and actions. This has led to broad misconceptions of God that have caused an even greater identity crisis in the world.

Many in the church and even in secular society have made unfounded judgments against God. The church and society have sought to place restrictions on God in an effort to make Him suitable for our lifestyles and needs. But God cannot be confined to our finite ideas and wisdom. We have certain conceptions about God based on what we have been taught, our experiences, and our observations, and we have certain assumptions about God that create barriers to true intimacy with Him. And intimacy with God is where our identity is proved and secured. I believe these judgments against God and assumptions we hold against Him are part of the reason that revival tarries. We do not spend enough time getting to know the God we represent. We do not rest enough in the secret place of God's presence so our identity can be shaped. We are not intentional enough about allowing God to teach us His perspective on our identity and His.

But thanks be to God; there is a cry arising in this hour—a cry for more of God, a cry to know more of Him and the power of His resurrection, a cry to fellowship with Him in life and death. This yearning for more is really a call to understand God's identity. Our journey to understanding God's identity will require us to confront the origins of our ideas about God, dismantle them with God's truth, and pursue God's revelation of His identity. Then and only then will we be prepared to receive God's outpouring of revelation and power in our lives.

This is what this book is about—you coming into the knowledge of your identity by first understanding God's identity. It is a book for world changers—individuals who know they have been called to change their cities, their families, and their lives but have yet to surrender to the fact that without God they cannot effectively accomplish this call. This book is for anyone who wants to set the record straight that God has an identity, that He does not want to be known as a higher power or be confined to our limited understandings and judgments of Him. It is for those who want to know the name of God and most importantly want to know God as He desires to be known—as Abba.

May this book bring great clarity, deliverance, and healing to your life. I pray that as you read this book, the revelation of God's identity and yours takes you on a new trajectory that will align you with the heart of the Father. I declare your heart's cry for more of God will be answered in this season. I prophesy that God will be made known to you as Abba, your Father, and that you will be found inseparable from Him. I prophesy that you will see what Abba sees, that you will know Abba as protector, that the will of Abba will be done in your life, and that from this moment on you will live as God's son or daughter.

1

THE "I AM THAT I AM"

Abba's Identity

"And God said unto Moses, I Am That I Am: and he said, Thus shalt thou say unto the children of Israel, I Am hath sent me unto you."

∞∞∞ EXODUS 3:14 ∞∞∞

IN THIS HOUR there is more of God. There is more of God that we need and want. We want to experience more of God, see more of Him, and be baptized in more of His glory, more of His power, and more of His love. We want to see revival that brings more souls into His kingdom.

If you have been paying attention to music trends over the past five years, you may have noticed that the Spirit of God has been breathing on psalmists and poets, pointing them in the direction of this need for more of

Him. I have never heard so many songs about wanting more! We have sung lyrics asking for more of God's Spirit, declaring our thirst for more of God's living water, and announcing the desire of our souls to overflow with more of God.

I believe this need for more of God is a direct response to a world that is in the middle of an identity crisis. There have been drastic shifts in gender and sexual identity, marriage identity, and even national identity. The news emerging from our geopolitical and socioeconomic structures bears witness to our need for more of God. We have taken identity formation into our own hands, and what this theft has accomplished is a vacuum of security and purpose on the earth. God's creation is desperate for a deeper revelation of God's identity. We need His identity branded on our hearts to accomplish the kingdom mandate on our lives, individually and collectively as the body of Christ.

God wants to reveal more of Himself to us. The Bible tells us that what brings God high glory is to be seen throughout the earth. He has a history of answering requests for more of Him. Take Moses, for example. As Exodus 33:18 states, Moses asked to see more of God's glory if the condition of favor had been met. God responded by saying that no one could see Him in all of His glory and live (v. 20). Where God is seen, flesh dies. But because Moses had found favor with God, God accommodated his request by allowing him to see a glimpse of Himself (from the back) (vv. 21–23). Moses was physically changed because of that one glimpse (Exod. 34:29).

If God is willing, then what is delaying this greater revelation of Him on the earth? I believe we have not received a greater revelation of who God is because we have not allowed the glimpses of God that we have seen to change us. The fact that if asked, we could name at least five carnally driven Christian believers proves that most people are not mentally ready to see God. They are unwilling to die to themselves to have the greater outpouring of God that they sing and pray about. Further, we are attempting to use our outdated ideas of who God is as a measuring rod of what more of God looks like.

To receive a deeper revelation of who God is, we must first resolve that He is not our ideas of Him. We must assess how we have defined God up to this point and address our misconceptions of Him. This goes for each of us individually and the church as a whole. Each of us has to examine our definitions of, fears about, and experiences with God. The more we confront the flaws in our definitions, expectations, and conclusions about God's identity, the more prepared we are to receive more than just a glimpse of God. Let's go further in our investigation of how we have misidentified God's identity, which limits God's outpour in our lives.

"I Am Not Your Definitions of Me"

Our hearts are filled with experiences, beliefs, and judgments that shape our definitions of others—who we know them to be, what their nature is, and how we expect them to behave. The accuracy of these definitions and perspectives of others is entirely dependent on how far we are willing to grow in intimacy and vulnerability with them. In the same way the level of intimacy we experience with God tends to shape our definitions of and beliefs about Him. These definitions shape what we believe about His nature, about what He will or will not do, and about what He is capable of accomplishing. The truth, however, is that God is not our personalized definitions of Him. In fact, those definitions are the very things that keep us from receiving the fresh revelation of God we desire.

Jesus was committed to revealing Himself as the Word of God. This consistent narrative would serve as an important reminder to us of just how serious God is about what He says, particularly what He says about Himself. We cannot define God apart from knowing His Word. To receive the revelation of God we cry out for, we must make a commitment to intentionally emptying our hearts of the perspectives and belief systems that were formed apart from the knowledge of what He has said about Himself, and we must strengthen our commitment to allowing the Word of God to reveal God's identity.

"I Am Not a Higher Power"

Our ideas of God do not just come from our personal definitions of Him. They can be influenced by the opinions of others too, whether they belong to God or His enemy. For example, over the last twenty years humanism and secularism have sought to define God as a higher power, the universe, or energy. Even Christian believers sometimes refer to God by these terms. By far the most egregious misclassification of God is as a higher power. Let me explain why.

The idea of God as *a* higher power suggests there is a hierarchy, and that positions God as equal in divine nature and strength to other powers with lesser divine powers beneath them. The issue with this humanistic approach to God is that it obscures the reality that He has no divine equal and is far above any created thing. Furthermore, nowhere in the Scriptures do we see God refer to Himself as a higher power. Whenever we subscribe to these generic and broad definitions of God, it wins us the right to live generic and broad lives. The idea of a "higher power" does not even begin to translate the standards God desires for us to live by. This broad language actually gives us the liberty to craft any combination of principles that satisfy our personal standards, even if they offend God. This is why some Christians can be comfortable with adopting ideas of God from Muslims, Buddhists, Hare Krishnas, Marcus Garvey's ideals, or anyone else who claims to have had an awakening from a "higher power" as a framework for understanding God. To regard God as He has revealed Himself through His Word is to espouse the responsibility of His expectations for us. We only come to know these expectations through His Word.

The idea of God as a higher power suggests that He is so big that His nature cannot be captured by a singular definition. This means He is not only a higher power but also the universe, the stars, Mother Nature, Mother Earth, and Mufasa and Simba from Disney's *The Lion King*. Following this line of thought, God is then the rocks and pebbles of the streams, trees, and eagles. God is "abstract"; God is everything, and everything is God.

God tells us who He is in the Scriptures. He is a person, not a higher power. God is the only true and wise God; besides Him there is no other power. In the Book of Exodus God communicates to His people, "I am the Lord. My name is Jealous" (Exod. 34:14, author's paraphrase). It is clear that He wants to be known how He wants to be known. Therefore we must put aside contemporary conceptions of and labels for God that not only discredit His sovereignty but also limit His inherent power. If we are going to have a greater revelation of God's identity, then we have to divorce ourselves from cultural and humanistic definitions of God.

"I AM NOT YOUR FEARS"

Many people who desire more of God cannot receive more of Him because of the lens of fear through which they view God. We all can admit to having fear. Fear is common, but when it is left unaddressed, it will prevent us from seeing the true identity of God. Fear comes in various forms. One is based on distorted expectations of or beliefs about God. The other is based on past traumatic experiences that dictate how we view God. Ultimately in whichever form it comes, fear creates a barrier to receiving and encountering the greater revelation of God's love.

Despite the cry for more of God some have a fear of God rooted in a distorted expectation. Sometimes this comes from fear-based evangelism, in which people are taught that they should become Christians solely so they do not go to hell. This gives people the wrong view about the fullness of God's identity because out of fear they just see Him as fire insurance to keep them out of hell. Even though hell is a reality, when people come into Christianity only because they fear God will send them to hell if they do not believe in Christ, it creates a distorted expectation that God is solely into punishment and should be feared. When individuals see God only through the fears of their distorted expectations that He is all about punishment, they become motivated by punishment. Therefore they live their lives with fear in the driver's seat and ride only in the lane of mercy. They become reliant on mercy to keep them from the punishment that they falsely believe God is looking to hand out to them. They miss out on the promises of verses such as 1 John 4:18, which says, "There is no fear in love. But perfect love drives out fear, because fear has to do with punishment. The one who fears is not made perfect in love" (NIV). When fear is at work in people's lives, they miss out on the promise that God is motivated by love and God is love—an understanding of God's identity that would empower them to let the love of God drive their lives freely into lanes of grace, righteousness, peace, and joy, as His Spirit desires.

Some have a distorted belief about God rooted in fear because of what they think God might require of them. I meet a lot of people Satan has deceived by causing them to think they should fear fully surrendering to God, radically obeying Him, and giving total lordship to Him. They fear doing so will cost them too much or that somehow they will miss out on something in life. This distorted belief, rooted in the fear of the unknown and self-preservation, places limitations on intimacy and communication with God.

If you hold this inaccurate understanding of God, consistent prayer and worship may often be very hard because you are afraid of what God will require of you. You may stay out of His presence and out of earshot so you do not hear what He has to say because it may require something of you that you are afraid of giving up. The issue with this is that in God's presence is where He releases more of Himself and His identity. As Christians the more committed we are to holding on to our fears from distorted expectations and beliefs about God, the more we restrict ourselves from seeing and knowing God.

Past traumatic experiences and even generational fear paint an unrealistic picture of God. Traumas we experience in life—such as grief, molestation, abuse, divorce of parents, or betrayal—open doorways of pain in our hearts. Pain from traumatic experiences finds medicine in fear, or in other words, fear may be used as a protective measure. So, for example, someone who has been betrayed may fear loving people because she does not want to be betrayed again. Often men are taught to toughen up and not cry out of fear of becoming too emotional. Fears from trauma will cause people to live guarded lives in an effort to keep themselves safe. Sometimes victims of trauma will refuse to let anyone, even God, protect them because they vowed to protect themselves after rape, molestation, or abuse. These fears caused by trauma give individuals a lens through which to view life. Some will view life as broken because of a broken marriage. Others will view life as empty because of the emptiness brought on by the sudden loss of a loved one.

Inevitably these lenses of fear are applied to God. Loving God becomes hard for some because they fear He will be separated from them, just as their divorced parents were when they were children. Some fear getting into God's presence because He will force them to do something they do not want to do, just as an abuser did in the past. These fears skew people's vision of God, and they cloud the truth of who God really is and how God loves, protects, and honors them.

Unresolved traumatic experiences that create a skewed lens are often passed down from one generation to another. For example, a grandmother who is burned in a relationship may cope with the trauma by developing a fear that every man will cheat on her. She passes along this fear to her daughter, saying, "Be careful with your husband around other women. Men cannot be trusted, and you better save up for a rainy day because you never know what your husband will wake up one day and do." The grandmother's fear is passed down to the mother, who passes these same fears down to her children, and the cycle continues throughout the generations if not met with the truth of God's identity. Certainly this fear of trusting the intentions and promises of men creates a lens through which God's intentions and promises seem to be untrustworthy, as if He will not keep a promise. Ultimately this fear is reinforced in how each daughter in this family views her own identity. Fear will say, "You are not smart enough to discern the intentions and promises of others, so stay away from the promises of God and others." The cycle of fear can affect men as well, who may be raised to not trust other men; deep relationships and bonds of community cannot be forged because they were taught, out of fear, that other men cannot be trusted. This fear of trusting other men creates a lens through which God's desire for relationship seems to be untrustworthy or inauthentic. Fear will say, "You can only trust yourself," and rob you of covenant relationships with God and others. Generational fear within our bloodlines causes our lenses to be darkened not just in how we view others and ourselves but also in how we view God.

When our view of God is through fear, Paul reminds us, it is as if we see God "through a glass, darkly" (1 Cor. 13:12). Fear is the darkest glass we could view God through because it perverts God's identity and our ability to believe what God says about Himself. When we see Him incorrectly, we respond to Him incorrectly, we believe Him incorrectly, and we obey Him incorrectly because the fears from our distorted expectations, beliefs, traumas, or generational cycles teach us incorrectly. The fears teach us things such as God is cruel, distant, and untrustworthy. However, God is not our fears. We must confront every fear in our hearts if we are to know God as He truly is and receive more of Him. The clearer our vision becomes of God, the greater our faith becomes to receive more of God, that which He desires to give to us. Confronting fear will be difficult, but the promise at the end of 1 Corinthians 13:12 is that our commitment to exchanging our lenses of fear for truth will allow us to experience the full revelation of God.

"I AM NOT MY ACTIONS"

God is neither our definition of Him nor a higher power. He certainly is not our fears. Here is something even more powerful that still does not define Him: God is not His actions. We cannot define God based solely on what He does. Certain populations of Christians and nonbelievers use God's judgment against Sodom and Gomorrah, for example, as the basis of their complete understanding of God. They have hijacked these and other similar stories and have used them to limit people's understanding of God. Yet the Bible tells us that God is more than His actions of justice and judgment. When we see God only as the judge who burned down Sodom and Gomorrah, we miss the aspect of God where He said He is "the LORD God, merciful and gracious, long-suffering, and abundant in goodness and truth, keeping mercy for thousands, forgiving iniquity and transgression and sin" (Exod. 34:6–7).

God's judgment and mercy may seem contradictory if we study only His actions and not His words. If our pursuit of more of God is anchored in His actions alone, our expectations of Him have already given us a flawed view. Our pursuit of the Lord must begin with the understanding that God is not His actions. God is so much more than anything we can ever conceptualize. Even with everything God has done, He still promises that He will remain the same. Our guarantee is that if we pursue God based on what He has said about Himself rather than what we saw Him do, we will have more of God than we could ever imagine. God wants us to know Him by what He *said*, which is why He sent His

Son, Jesus Christ, the Word of God. Christ came so we would know God's personality and to limit the risk of people misquoting God.

"I AM NOT YOUR EXPERIENCES"

Part of the challenge involved in receiving more of God is our experiences. While this is not devilish, demonic, or evil, it does put us at a disadvantage. We are limited because our experiences are not reliable sources of information. Our experiences have the power to lie to us; our experiences have the power to hide the truth of God, not to mention our experiences do not have the power to reveal God's motives and intentions. So when we act as if our personal truth is a matter of fact rather than flexible and negotiable, we are already operating in error.

The Bible does not define God by experiences of Him, yet many of us take our personal experiences as our litmus test to measure how much more of God we can receive. We desire more of God in our hearts but only want the more to be like the feeling we had when we first got saved. We pray for more but only want the more to look like our experience of receiving the baptism of the Holy Spirit. We cry out for more but only want God's more to look like whatever mountaintop moment we experienced with God.

As Matthew 17 records, Peter, James, and John had a mountaintop experience in which they got to see God's glory reveal Jesus as the fulfillment of the Law of Moses and the prophecies of the prophets. In this experience, which is known as the Transfiguration, Peter's first inclination was to build a monument. However, God had so much more in store for Peter. Peter wanted to build a tabernacle, but God wanted to use Peter to build the church. If God could have been defined only by that one experience Peter had on the Mount of Transfiguration, the church of Jesus Christ never would have been formed. There is more to God than our past experiences. There is more to God than Him paying our bills, healing our bodies, and providing our salvation. Your experiences with God are important and necessary for your relationship with Him. They should not, however, form an expectation that God can or will only move in ways we have experienced in the past. Our experiences of God should not become the definition of God's identity. God does not want us to just stay in our past experiences; He wants to give us more! The desire of God, as 2 Corinthians 3:18 tells us, is to take us from one glorious experience to infinitely more.

Sometimes it is not our experiences but the experiences of others that limit the more of God in our lives. For example, if you grew up in the church, your experiences often have to do with or are related to someone else's experiences of God. We often say things such as, "I remember when Big Mama used to raise her hands like this," "Deacon Rob prayed like this," or "Pastor said this to our children's choir Sunday." All these examples have to do with someone else defining your experiences with God. Their experiences with God do not have to dictate how you lift your hands in worship, pray, or define His identity. When you take the experiences of others as the measurement for how God can move in your life, it causes you to be thrown off when you learn God is not who others said He is or that their theology of God was based on an understanding formed by their generation as opposed to God's Word.

If we were to limit God to the religious experiences of others, imagine the type of lives and churches we would be forced to lead and attend. If you are a woman, you might have to sit in a church with a skirt down to your ankles, your head covered in a wrap, and no makeup on your face. These churches most likely would have a whole theology based on their reading of scriptures such as 1 Corinthians 11:2–16 to teach that God is extremely distracted by women's clothing and hair and the lipstick they wear at church. However, in these verses Paul was speaking to the limitations of the Greco-Roman-Jewish culture of the time, in which hair worn down and loose would suggest a woman of questionable morals. Therefore kidnapping this set of verses or someone's experience with God and making it the sole basis for our understanding of God's identity or our own identity causes us to become hostages to the limitations of the context of that experience and causes us to miss out on the more of God's freedom and identity.

We cannot take the limitations or experiences of others and place them on God and call it theology. Theology comes from the truth of God's identity. And the truth is that God is very decided in His identity. He is decided in His desire to grant us more of Him, and He is decided in the fact that our identity should be drawn from Him. The limitations that religion wants to place on God's identity is an attack not only on women. Men may be allowed to go to church only when they wear what the church deems the right attire because experiences caused them to believe that God is disinterested in their souls if they wear the wrong things to church. Yet the truth is whether we are male or female, God is not distracted by our outward appearances; Jesus said God is concerned with our hearts. (See Matthew 15:15–20.) God is concerned with our belief of the truth of His identity in our hearts. So many people miss out on the full revelation of God's identity because they are trying to box God in to the experiences of the past. But God does not want us to be so focused on our outward appearance or the religious experiences of others that we completely miss the truth of His identity.

God does not want to be boxed in by our experiences or the experiences of others. John 4:24 records Jesus telling us that "God is a Spirit." If God is a spirit, then He cannot be confined to an experience. Jesus goes on in the rest of the verse to say that because God is a spirit, we must worship Him both in spirit and in truth. So our pursuit of more of God has to be rooted in the truth of God rather than our experiences. God wants us to know that He is not our experiences of Him. God comes to liberate us into something even greater than one-off experiences. He comes to liberate us into consistent relationship with Him.

When we divest ourselves of our judgments of God that were based on our own experiences or the experiences of others, we position ourselves to encounter God's truth, which aligns us with how God desires for us to see Him.

"I AM NOT THE SAME AS YOUR EARTHLY EXAMPLE"

God desires to release more of His presence so we can see Him face-to-face. He desires to answer our cries for Him, but as we have established, our definitions, limitations, expectations, and judgments hinder us from seeing more of God. In addition, our conclusions, or the inferences we have made concerning God, are also limiting the outpour of God upon our lives. These conclusions that we draw about God's abilities and capabilities are often based on our earthly examples of authority, such as our natural or adoptive father, a grandparent, a sibling, or even a mentor or coach.

The issue with drawing conclusions about God from our earthly examples is that if we encountered inconsistency in a natural parent, betrayal by a boss, or a pastor who was disinterested in investing in us or unwilling to do so, we project that image upon God. We draw conclusions and come to believe inaccurate things, such as God will be inconsistent in His dealing with us because our parents were inconsistent in loving or protecting us. We draw conclusions that God will not be faithful because others in authority betrayed us. We may even be tempted to conclude that God is too busy to help us and disinterested in our issues. When we draw conclusions about God based on earthly examples of authority, it will cause us to cry out for more of God, but we are only really getting more of the same! That is because our conclusions based on earthly examples keep us from seeing the truth of God's identity. Our conclusions seek to hold God hostage to our interpretations of Him, so that is how we will look for God's more to manifest in our lives. Our hearts may cry out for more but not trust that God will answer us consistently, faithfully, and despite our circumstances. This is the definition of insanity: we do the same thing—project our earthly examples upon God—and somehow expect a different conclusion—to experience more of God. This is impossible. We have to confess that God is not akin to our earthly examples. Numbers 23:19 says, "God is not a man, that he should lie; neither the son of man, that he should repent." We must forsake every idea and notion that God will be similar to any human being whom we have encountered on the earth because He is God.

"I AM THAT I AM"

Now that you know who God is not, you may be wondering what God's identity is and why it matters. God's identity matters to us because our identity and the identity of the church is found in Him. To get more of God—more of His peace, provision, love, and power—we have to have the proper view of God and understand His identity. If the way we see God is distorted, then inevitably the way we see ourselves will be distorted. Therefore understanding our individual identity does not begin with us; it begins with God. It is found in the God who told Moses, as recorded in Exodus 3:14, that He is "I AM THAT I AM." In the next couple of chapters we will work together to explore God's identity and learn more about the God whose name is "I Am That I Am."

2

OUR LOVING FATHER

Beloved Children

"After this manner therefore pray ye: Our Father which art in heaven, hallowed be thy name."

∞∞∞ MATTHEW 6:9 ∞∞∞

ALL OF GOD's nature and faculties were captured by one name: I Am. This is the name God introduces Himself to Israel with, and it encapsulated everything. When the Israelites needed a judge, I Am was a judge. When they needed a home, I Am created a nation for them and was a ruler. He was also El Shaddai, the almighty and all-sufficient One who sustained Israel for generations. The Old Testament is filled with these descriptions of the nature and character of God recorded by men and women who were inspired by the Holy Spirit to speak for and about God. Perhaps the most important revelation of the Old Testament for a people immersed in a culture of many gods was that the I Am is the only living God!

God's supremacy and authorship of creation was summed up in this one statement to Pharaoh through Moses: "Thus shalt thou say unto the children of Israel, I Am hath sent me unto you" (Exod. 3:14). We see this truth echoed in the Law God would later give to Moses. "I am the LORD thy God" were the first words etched into the tablets (Exod. 20:2). "Thou shalt have no other gods before me" (v. 3). In His showdown with Pharaoh, who represented the highest of all the world's systems and its gods, I Am reigned as the undisputed champion. As God closed out the Old Testament, I Am began a conversation with Israel about the most powerful aspect of His identity. God declared: "Behold, I will send you Elijah the prophet before the coming of the great and dreadful day of the LORD: And he shall turn the heart of the fathers to the children, and the heart of the children to their fathers, lest I come and smite the earth with a curse" (Mal. 4:5–6). God left the people with a promise concerning fathers and sons and declared that if this promise was not fulfilled, a curse would overtake the earth. Then I Am silenced Himself for four hundred years.

THE FATHER REVEALED

Four hundred years later a Son was born in a manger in Bethlehem, and His name was Jesus. At Jesus's baptism God announced, "This is my beloved Son, in whom I am well pleased" (Matt. 3:17). Traditionally we only approach the importance of this statement from the perspective of Jesus, the Son. However, this statement was the fulfillment of the promise God made at the end of the Old Testament (found in Malachi 4:5–6) before the four hundred years of silence that fathers' hearts would be turned to their children. "This is my beloved Son, in whom I am well pleased" was God's way of revealing Himself as Father to humanity!

Think about it. Jesus needed no further validation of His identity. His presence on the earth was validation enough of His embodiment of prophecy fulfilled. The prophet Isaiah declared that Jesus's name would be called "Wonderful, Counsellor, The mighty God, The everlasting Father, The Prince of Peace" (Isa. 9:6). God went even further to establish Jesus's identity before His arrival by saying, "Therefore the Lord himself shall give you a sign; Behold, a virgin shall conceive, and bear a son, and shall call his name Immanuel" (Isa. 7:14). God had given all the clues and markers to Jesus's identity before He was born on the earth, so when Jesus was baptized and the Father made His statement, He was not confirming to Jesus who He was because Jesus was already resolute in His identity. Furthermore, by the time of Jesus's baptism, He was thirty years old. God had been working His identity and His assignment in Him since the beginning. Thus, "this is my beloved Son, in whom I am well pleased" was God's introduction of Himself as Father.

Why was this introduction necessary? Recall that there was a four-hundred-year period when God was silent. Generations lived and generations died having heard nothing directly from the Lord. When Jesus lived, all those who would have known the Lord's voice had died, along with their definitions, limitations, expectations, judgments, experiences, and ideas of God. Therefore it was important that God reintroduce Himself not only as I Am but as Father—Father God.

When Jesus was baptized, the heavens opened (Matt. 3:16). Why did the heavens need to open if God was only confirming Jesus's identity? If the statement was just Jesus's affirmation, then, some can argue, only Jesus needed to hear it. But everyone heard the voice.[1] It was one of the rare times when God spoke with an audible voice, and it was not restricted to a prophet.

The reintroduction of God as Father was necessary because of a prophetic statement that was behind this audible announcement from God. God's identity as Father was the only way we could understand the events between Matthew and Revelation. Without the understanding of God as Father, we cannot fully understand the stories of the New Testament. Apart from understanding God as Father, we cannot understand any of the Gospels, appreciate the Book of Acts, receive the revelation of grace in Paul's writings, recognize the body of Christ, or envision what John saw on the island of Patmos. Remember, the last thing the people understood about God was that He was angry, disgusted, and disappointed with a people who failed to meet His standard. He judged them and turned them over to the creatures of the field and the beasts. Malachi 4, the last Scripture passage of the Old Testament, was about a curse. Most likely this was the image people had of God.

The most fascinating part of God's revelation as Father is that if I had written the Bible, I would have placed it at the end. I would have made this the bottom line, the finishing move of God. However, to delay that revelation would not have provided a pathway for those who had not experienced the God who answered by fire and displayed certain fatherly attributes in past times to connect to God as Father. This is why God starts the New Testament story by saying, "This is my beloved Son, in whom I am well pleased." The opening of the New Testament with God introducing Himself as Father *was* the finishing move for God after all—prophecy fulfilled. It was about God the Father intercepting the curse upon humanity through Christ, His Son, so we would choose to turn our hearts to God and declare that He is indeed a good Father.

"I AM NOT THE SAME AS YOUR NATURAL FATHER"

This concept of God as Father was hard for many to understand. Look at John 10:30–31; it says the Jews began to pick up rocks to stone Jesus to death when He called God Father. This concept of God as our Father is still hard for many to grasp today because they are placing the definitions, limitations, expectations, judgments, and conclusions of their natural fathers upon God. To understand the fullness of the promise Jesus fulfilled in His life and to experience more of God's identity as Father, we must first declare that God is not our natural father. You may have had a great relationship with your father. Your natural father may have provided a good example of fatherhood. This is wonderful, but even natural fathers are flawed and can make mistakes. God is the only perfect Father! Even with a good example of an earthly father, you must cast off your ideas of how God the Father will behave toward you and your comparisons of Him and your natural father if you want to receive more of Him.

It is hard for some of us to receive God as our Father because of the way in which our natural fathers defined *father* for us through their actions, or lack thereof. Natural fathers ideally guide us toward understanding our identity and purpose. That is what happened for Adam in the garden; God gave Adam identity and purpose. God was Adam's Father and by extension the Father of the whole human race. However, Adam presented an imperfect picture of God the Father to his children once sin entered his heart. Adam, like all natural fathers, was a human being who had flaws. These flaws were passed down through bloodlines and became the foundation by which we seek to relate to God as Father.

Then there are those who have experienced betrayal by their fathers. I happen to think there is no greater betrayal than to have a man responsible for your protection, provision, and identity take advantage of you. There are many who experienced betrayal in the form of abandonment and rejection by an absentee father, but others have experienced it through sexual, physical, and verbal abuse at the hands of a very present father or father figure. These violations, both abandonment and abuse, dismantle trust toward a father. So by the time God says, "Hello, I am your Father," it is natural to understand why individuals who have experienced betrayal by a father pull away and harden or brace their hearts for the worst. You may be OK with God as a Creator because that matches your experience of a natural father who was interested only in creating his children and not caring for them. You may even be OK with God as a gift giver if your natural father was present only at birthdays; you can accept a God who blesses you without conditions and does not require you to follow his standards and instructions. Maybe your dad was present but a distant authoritarian. Thus, you are OK with God as a redeemer of your soul; you view Him as an overbearing dictator who is always looking for a chance to punish you when you mess up. Even though these ideas might be easier to accept, accepting God as Father can be hard if your natural father betrayed you. These ideas of your natural father are stopping you from receiving the revelation of God as Father in your heart. It is stopping you because you feel that your natural father was unfixable, unredeemable, unlovable, or unfit. Somehow that image of your natural father has been projected to God. However, God wants you to know that He is not your natural father.

When we choose to keep the reflection of our natural fathers as the only way we view God, we have created an idol in our hearts. Idols can start out of an authentic desire to understand God's identity, but they only end up as a physical or metaphorical graven image that is built on a false identity of God. These false versions of God are rooted in assumptions, small glimpses, or ideas of God's identity, but their sole purpose is to block God's true identity from being revealed in our hearts. This is why God is not a reflection of your natural father! Your natural father is an imperfect reflection of God, a graven image at best of God the Father. In the New Testament, through Jesus God establishes that He is not a reflection at all. God is God. He wants His identity to be known to us as Father.

To receive the fullness of this revelation of God's identity as Father, you are going to have to put down the ideas of the past pains, hurts, rejection, and trauma you may have experienced at the hand of your natural father. In gratitude you will also have to commit to laying down even the good memories you have of your natural father. There must be a purposing of your heart to come out of agreement with the plans of Satan to distort your view of God's identity. You will not be the first or the last on this journey. People such as Abraham, Elisha, Ruth, and Paul had to leave the pains and responsibilities of natural families to enter into a more perfect relationship with God. They had to leave behind what they knew for a greater revelation. In the same way, you need to divorce your past relationship with your ideas of a father. This is your moment; let go of the past, and enter into a union with God the Father.

A LOVING FATHER

When God the Father set the record straight and spoke up for Himself about who He is, the heavens opened over Jesus and shut again. It was an open door, per se, for Jesus to fulfill His purpose. Saving us from sin is not all Jesus was called to accomplish on the earth. Saving us from sin was a consequence of Jesus's birth, life, ministry, and death, but it was not the only thing He came to do. "So what was the purpose of the heavens opening and Jesus coming to the earth?" you may ask. It was to reveal the Father. The purpose of Jesus's thirty-three years of ministry was not just to save us from sin. He could have done that quickly. Saving us from sin was easier than revealing the Father to us. He took thirty-three years to reveal God as Father and three days to save us from sin. When He was casting out devils, He was not saving us from sin. When He was healing the sick, He was not saving us from sin. When He was preaching on the mountains, He was not saving us from sin. It took all of three days—just seventy-two hours—to win the war on sin and to save our souls. However, it took thirty-three years for Jesus to show us the dimensions of the Father, whom He called Abba.

Jesus demonstrated to us that Abba is a loving Father who invests in, provides for, listens to, and hopes for His children. As recorded in John 3:16, Jesus told us, "For God so loved the world, that he gave his only begotten Son, that whosoever believeth in him should not perish, but have everlasting life." Jesus revealed that Abba is love and He loves us. He loves you so much that He was willing to invest His only begotten Son into the earth so the human race would not be without the love of the Father! Jesus's life shows us the reality of Abba's ability to provide for us. When Jesus lived on the earth, He had everything He needed. He found money in the fish's mouth (Matt. 17:27). He had access to an abundant supply of food. He could send His disciples for a donkey and have one be present when they arrived (Matt. 21:2, 6–7). We also learn through Jesus's life that Abba not only speaks but also listens. You never see Jesus praying twice about the same thing. God heard Him every time He said something. That is the power of a life lived under an open heaven of a loving Father who declares, "This is my beloved Son [or daughter], in whom I am well pleased." Abba hears us. Abba grants to us what we ask, just as Jesus saw the manifestation of what He declared.

We can be assured that Abba is not a theory. Abba is a person, a loving Father who has hopes, thoughts, and emotions for His children. Abba hopes that all of creation will come into the knowledge of Him through His Son. He has thoughts of peace, not of evil, and to bring us to an expected end. Our Father grieves when the investment of His Son is not received on the earth and His creation has to be subjected to torment and punishment. He is grieved when the people He believes in and hopes for are tormented in hell, where they chose to spend eternity. Abba is saddened that their actions put them there despite the expected end He desires. This is a grievance for God because His hope is that none "should perish, but that all should come to repentance," according to 2 Peter 3:9. God does not want anyone to live an eternity apart from Him. Yet as a loving father does for his children, God grants us the freedom to make our own choices.

In addition to grieving, Abba also rejoices. He is joyful and filled with glory when we use our free will to live as His Word trains us without His having to force us. God rejoices when we put down assumptions of Him and receive the revelation of Him as Father. Abba rejoices when we see Him as a loving Father. Abba Father is the perfect balance of everything true and right in a father. He extends an invitation to you today for a renewed relationship with Him as Father.

PURSUE RELATIONSHIP

Abba's invitation to let go of the past and grab hold of a future under His fatherly protection can seem intimidating or uncertain. The good news is that Jesus is our perfect model of how to relate to and embrace God as Father. Jesus teaches us that the best way to relate to God as Father is to pursue relationship with Him. Pursuing relationship with Abba as Father starts with what I call the three Cs: consistent communication, clarity, and casting your cares. First we must be consistent in our conversations with God so we can learn who He is as our Father. We must seek clarity from Abba. Then we are to cast our cares on our Father daily. These practical steps will help you build and develop a strong relationship with God as Father.

Consistent communication

There is a tremendous amount of power in communication. Communication is an absolutely indispensable tool when you desire to relate to someone. Conversations have the power to build trust, create meaning, and engage others. Conversations allow for learning and provide a basis for understanding to occur. Therefore to relate to Abba as Father, we must be willing to dedicate ourselves to communicating with God. We have to be willing to enter into conversations with Abba that will provide opportunities for us to learn about His identity as a Father. We have to begin conversations with God that will allow us to understand, trust, and engage with Him as Father. Not only do we have to communicate with Abba, but we also must do so consistently. Without consistent communication, there is no way for the information God is sharing with us to infiltrate our lives.

The disciples took notice of the intimate relationship of Jesus with Abba and attributed it to His consistent communication with the Father. They noticed that Jesus was in constant communication with God through prayer. So, as Luke 11:1 records, the disciples asked Jesus to teach them how to pray. They wanted to know how to pursue relationship with God and relate to Him. Jesus gave them a pattern for communicating with the Father that today we call the Lord's Prayer. The first thing Jesus said to them, as recorded in Matthew 6:9, is "therefore pray ye: Our Father which art in heaven, hallowed be thy name." Right at the top—right where it belongs—Jesus says if you want to embrace God's invitation to an intimate relationship, then communicate with Him as Abba, your Father.

Communicating with God using Jesus's model of prayer reminds us to make the communication personal by calling God Father (Luke 11:2). *Hallow*, found in the prayer, means "to honor or give respect." We honor God by coming to Him with a desire to be in relationship with Him, by wanting to speak with Him, by acknowledging that God is Abba Father, and by saying good things to Him about Himself, such as when we say: "Abba, You are good. Father, You are wonderful. God, there is no one like You." Our words of praise, thanksgiving, and affirmation help us give God the rightful position in our hearts as Father. We give respect to God not just by talking but also by stopping and listening for Abba's thoughts. Often people will feel as if God is distant or not answering them, and that is because they are not taking the time to listen. We are not called to have a one-sided conversation with God. Abba wants to have conversations with us that build a relationship. This requires both sides to take the appropriate moments to speak. We can speak, and then we must take time to listen to what God wants to communicate back to us by listening to our senses, to the Holy Spirit's leading, or to the wisdom of Scripture.

Another sign of honor, respect, admiration, and regard for God is found in our consistency in communicating with Him. Think about a romantic relationship; when the individuals first get together, they can spend hours on the phone communicating together. Consider the number of conversations best friends have had with each other. Constant communication is necessary because relationships are built on learning and understanding. The more we know about a person, the more we can trust him, the more we understand his identity, and the more we desire to engage with him. Our relationship with God adheres to the same principles. As a matter of fact, our conversations with God require even more consistency than those with a spouse or a friend because God is our Father and source of life. To be consistent, we must be firm in making the time to talk to the Father. Busyness or the inability to manage time will try to rob us of our consistency of communication with Abba. However, the more we practice coming into agreement with God as Father and honor Him as the head, the leader, the Father of our lives, the easier it will become to consistently communicate with Him and the more we will want to.

When we do not communicate with God consistently or honor, respect, and acknowledge God as Abba, our prayers are strictly provisionally based, need-based, reactionary to a trial or a crisis, or a response to an emotion. All these types of prayers are temporal and fleeting, and they relate to God in ways we see our natural fathers or how someone would treat an idol. This is why Jesus placed those temporal and fleeting things at the end of the Lord's Prayer, our model prayer. At the beginning Jesus placed the only constant He knew, and that is Abba, God our Father. Jesus knew it would help align the rest of our communication with God when we started our conversation with a rightful understanding of His identity as Father. Not only does communicating in prayer with God our Father help us align our hearts, but it also helps us hear and apply His truths in our lives.

Clarity

In our consistent communication with the Father we cannot be afraid to press in to God for moments of clarity. Moments of clarity help us pursue relationship with Abba because they give us information we can use to learn more about and understand our Father. As we acknowledge God as Father, we show respect to Him by asking Him questions about Himself. We can ask God questions about what He is like as a Father. We can ask Him what He likes and does not like. We can also ask Abba to teach us and help us understand His identity as a Father. We can ask God questions about His mind on a particular topic and His attitude on something we have seen on the news, heard in church, or experienced in worship. There is no question that is off-limits to our

Father. We can even ask His thoughts about us, and we can ask Abba about His plans for us, others, or even our city and nation.

In the model prayer that Jesus taught the disciples, He first told them to acknowledge God as Father because this helps us focus on God and get His attention. Starting prayer with the understanding that God is Father dictates what we believe He will and will not accomplish on our behalf. Once we acknowledge God as Father, then Jesus shows us that from there we can ask anything of God in His name (Luke 11:2–4; John 14:13). This is because acknowledging God as Father aligns our expectations and prepares us to hear God's clarity on any matter.

When you place Abba first, you can ask any question you like because His stance, His investment, His interest, His belief, and His confidence are postured toward you. Likewise when you pursue relationship with Abba through consistent communication, building a relationship in which you are not afraid to ask questions and seek clarity, your stance, your investment, your interest, your belief, and your confidence shift toward God. This allows your heart and mind to be open to hearing and receiving definite, transparent, and pure communication that comes from the Father with answers to every question.

Abba welcomes our questions of clarity because they not only build relationship with Him but also help God provide protection for us. Questions of clarity help provide protection for us by taking the guesswork out of our lives. We do not have to figure out the right decision on our own. We can simply ask God for clarity. He is able to provide protection for us by giving us wisdom and knowledge or understanding for our circumstances. This keeps us from harm, trial and error, and unnecessary heartbreak that comes from trying to figure out life on our own. We were meant to always ask God for clarity and trust that our Father would happily provide clarity for us. Abba is willing to provide clarity for us because protection is one of the traits of a father, and Abba longs to protect His children. Therefore when we ask God questions within our conversations, it allows Him to flex His nature as Father. When we do not ask God for clarity concerning His identity, our identity, or any matter, we rob ourselves of the opportunity to have our Father protect us. When we do not get clarity from Abba, it is like groping around in the darkness. God does not desire our relationship with Him to be blind. He wants us to be knowledgeable about Him as our Father and to live in the protection He provided. So in your consistent communication with God do not be afraid to ask God questions. Challenge yourself to ask God the questions that will unlock even more revelation and mysteries. Never feel as if you are bothering God or asking too many questions of Abba. He is your Father! For the Father your questions are a sign of respect, admiration, and regard for who He is as our Father.

Casting your cares

Finally, when relating to God as Father, we are to pursue relationship with Him by casting our cares upon Him. We cast our cares on Abba by giving Him the first right as our Father to attend to us, our concerns, and our circumstances. Jesus's instruction to start prayers with "our Father" first reminds us to cast the cares of life on Him first. When things become a worry, we are free to approach our Father and give Him all the details. Then He will give us the strength to leave our cares at His table for Him to take care of or to provide us with solutions we can implement. At this step of relationship building, it is much easier to cast our cares on Abba because through our consistent communication and our asking of questions and listening to gain clarity, we have built trust with God as our Father. Therefore, to cast our cares on the Father makes a statement about what we know about our strength and what we trust about His strength as our Father.

The casting of our cares on Abba also grants us benefits in our relationship with our Father. Psalm 55:22 says, "Cast thy burden upon the LORD, and he shall sustain thee: he shall never suffer the righteous to be moved." A deliberate discipline of casting our cares upon the Lord as we consistently communicate with Him provides security not just in our relationship with God but also in our hearts and minds. Casting our cares on God helps us sustain our relationship with Abba because doing so serves as a reminder of how much our Father cares about us and how much He cares for us. When we cast our cares on our Father God, we cast down our definitions, limitations, expectations, and conclusions. The truth is as we seek to relate to God as Father in our prayer lives, we unknowingly talk to God as if He is criticizing us and watching for us to commit an error, be flawed, or make a mistake. We pray as if He is watching us to see if we are deserving of an answer to our prayers. These thoughts place a restriction on our relationship with God as our

Father, but the deliberate discipline of casting our cares on Abba reminds us that He is a loving Father whose heart is turned toward us the minute we think to call out to Him.

Casting our cares on Abba helps us relate to Him as Father because we are reminded that He cares for us. He cares enough to want to help us remove the anxiety, worries, and unforgiveness that seek to hinder our ability to approach Him as Father. If we acknowledge God as Abba Father as a matter of discipline and something bothers us, we can surrender our care to Him and benefit from not being moved by the situations and circumstances of life. We can have confidence that God permanently ended our need to worry or be anxious for anything by sending His Son. We never have to try to relate to God as if we have everything together and can handle life and our issues on our own. The truth is any effort of our own will never be enough to fully solve all our insecurities, troubles, and stresses. The One who can help is God our Father, who cares for us and for our every need within relationship with Him.

WE ARE BELOVED

We are often taught that the cues for our identity come from our natural parents. Our personalities, character, and attributes seem to be drawn from those of our mother or father. The issue with this theory is those who grew up without one or both of their parents, had negative experiences with their parents, or had distant mothers and fathers are at a disadvantage. According to society these individuals are disadvantaged because they are not able to attribute their personality or character traits to someone. This disadvantage causes an identity crisis for many people. However, even if we all had both of our parents and had a great relationship with them, there would still be some personality and character traits we cannot attribute to them. This causes issues in our identity. Therefore our identity must have another source that is much more reliable and trustworthy. This is not to say that our race or ethnicity, gender, and specific talents, character traits, and personality do not contribute to who we are. Certainly they do. However, they are not the full story because there are definitions, limitations, expectations, judgments, and conclusions associated with these traits. In the same way that we must commit to putting down the ideas of the past concerning our natural fathers, we must also be willing to come out of agreement with fractures in our identity to receive the fullness of God's identity for our lives.

When you receive God as your Father and truly believe that Abba is your loving Father, God as Father becomes the consistent barometer for how you view your identity. In your pursuit of relationship with God the Father through consistent communication, clarity, and casting your cares upon Him, you will begin to see the genesis of your own identity. God is the source of your identity not only as your Creator but also as your Father. He calls you to draw your identity from His. If God is your loving Father, then your identity is rooted in His unconditional love. Your identity—the characteristics determining who you are as an individual—is that you are wholeheartedly loved by your Father God. When Abba looks at you, He identifies you as His beloved. You are the apple of His eye, an individual who is much loved. You are precious to Him. Jeremiah 31:3 says, "The LORD hath appeared of old unto me, saying, Yea, I have loved thee with an everlasting love: therefore with lovingkindness have I drawn thee." God's love for you has a history, as does your identity. That history is what makes God's love for you unconditional and confirms your identity as Abba's beloved.

God did not just start loving you when He saw your commitment to releasing your past ideas of Him. God's love is not just sometimes; it is unconditional. He does not wait to see if He likes who you turned out to be before He loves you and determines your identity is beloved. Jesus echoes this truth about your identity: "For God so loved the world, that he gave his only begotten Son, that whosoever believeth in him should not perish, but have everlasting life" (John 3:16). God made provisions to answer your question concerning your identity before you were born, much less before you were born again. This was Abba's way of helping you realize that despite all the things you chase to find your identity, He is the source of your identity and has been all along. From the source of His love and lovingkindness, through Jesus, your identity flows as unequivocally, unquestionably, totally, and completely loved. God was so sure of your identity that He was willing to invest His Son's life to prove it.

Satan's plan is for you to never be secure in God's identity as a loving Father, which consequently causes you to be insecure in your identity as God's beloved. His plan for you is to live with a broken identity and to never fully receive the revelation of God's identity as a loving

Father. The hope of the devil is that if you never see God as Abba, then you will never fully understand that how the world defines your identity is skewed. Satan's plan is for you to doubt Abba and Abba's Son, Jesus, so you are undecided, insecure, and unstable in your understanding of God's identity. If Satan can achieve his plan, you will be undecided, insecure, and shifted by every wind of doctrine, situation, or circumstance concerning your identity. This is why pursuing relationship with Abba as Father through consistent communication, clarity, and casting your cares upon God is so important. You can build the trust and reliability so you do not have to doubt God or your identity. Satan knows if you come into the realization of God as Abba Father and begin to understand the power that comes from the fact that God unconditionally loves you, then you will be unstoppable. Think about it—Jesus was the last person who was fully invested in God's identity as Abba Father. His unwavering acceptance of God's identity and His own identity as God's beloved caused Him to shift history forever! Thus, the devil works tirelessly to make you lose confidence in God's love for you, which ultimately causes you to lose confidence and hope in your identity as unconditionally loved.

If you show me someone who is feeling insecure, lacks confidence, and is depressed by every issue or circumstance in life, then I can show you a person who is not rooted in the full revelation of God as Abba Father or his identity as unconditionally loved. Show me someone who does not believe in God or is not fully committed to God as Abba, and I can show you a person who is likely undecided, insecure, and lacking confidence in his own identity as a person wholeheartedly loved by God. You never see Jesus doubting God as His Father or His identity as Abba's beloved. Yes, Jesus wrestled with the greatest sacrifice He would ever make, but He never doubted His identity—not even once. Remember when the devil came to test Jesus after forty days of fasting in the wilderness? Jesus was able to pass that test because He had confidence in Abba as His Father and confidence that God loved Him so much that Abba would protect Him. As a result Jesus had the confidence to withstand the temptations of Satan. (See Matthew 4:1–11.) Abba extends this same power Jesus had to withstand the enemy and win to all of us who open our hearts to fully receive God's identity as Father and our identity as God's beloved.

When you see God as Abba and relate to Him as Father by pursuing relationship with Him through consistent communication, clarity, and casting your cares on Him, you will have the confidence to live out your identity. When Abba's love shapes your identity, your cries for more of God manifest in limitless possibilities that affirm God's love for you as His beloved. The more you commit to overcoming every barrier in your past from your natural father and in your heart that causes you to push God the Father away, the more He is committed to drawing you near. As you lean into Him with constant communication and prayer, you will discover just how much He was already leaning toward you.

3

OUR LIBERATING FATHER

The Spirit of Adoption

*According as he hath chosen us in him before the
foundation of the world, that we should be holy and
without blame before him in love: Having predestinated
us unto the adoption of children by Jesus Christ to
himself, according to the good pleasure of his will.*

∞∞ Ephesians 1:4–5 ∞∞

GOD WANTS THE right to be our Abba. Although
we may be considered God's idea, a creation
originated from God, and even God's DNA as His creation, sin separated us from God and made us fatherless
orphans. When Adam and Eve fell into sin in the Garden
of Eden, it separated them from God, and they lost their
Father in God. This was not of God's choosing but was
of their choosing. Their lives had been characterized by

close intimacy with God the Father, even walking and talking with Him in the garden, but the sin nature drove them in fear to hide from the Father. The consequence of their choice to sin, explained in Genesis 3:16–19, was their enslavement to work, desires, and emotions. By an act of their will they chose to separate from Father God and hide, which introduced an orphan spirit.

Natural orphans are typically children who have lost their parents through death or abandonment. The orphan spirit refers to the spiritual condition of humanity when we lost our connection with God through our abandonment of Him and His identity. Unbelievers have an orphan spirit because they have not even acknowledged God, let alone recognized Him as their Father. We as Christians can have an orphan spirit when we profess outwardly to believe in God as our Father but choose to live as slaves to sin. We are also operating in the orphan spirit when we accept the idea of God as Father but don't live our lives as if He is our Father. Adam and Eve had walks and talks with God in the Garden of Eden. They had a relationship with Him, and yet they still chose to live as orphans, apart from God.

When Adam and Eve, through their sin, chose to separate from Father God, they became orphans. Whereas Father God provided protection, provision, and identity for them in the past, after they made their choice, they were left to themselves to create their own identity and toil for their own provision and protection. They lost their name and place with the Father. They were God's creation but lost their name of God's children. They were brought into bondage to labor, desires, and emotions and lost their space as rulers and leaders who were free to have dominion on the earth. Genesis 3:23–24 says, "Therefore the LORD God sent him forth from the garden of Eden, to till the ground from whence he was taken. So he drove out the man; and he placed at the east of the garden of Eden Cherubims, and a flaming sword which turned every way, to keep the way of the tree of life." Adam and Eve were driven from their place of residence in the garden to the wilderness of the earth. Through their sin we have all been subjected to a life as orphans apart from our Father and our home in the kingdom of God.

THE ARRIVAL OF THE KINGDOM

Adam and Eve sent the world into a total and complete identity crisis that we have been stumbling to emerge from ever since. There seemed to be no hope for Adam and Eve and thus no hope for us, human beings born into their lineage and bloodline. However, God spoke a promise, the promise that a child would be born (Gen. 3:15). So hopelessness gave way to hope as the Son of God came into the world to shed light on a dark situation. Those in a world dark and lost to the rejection, loneliness, alienation, fear, and isolation of an orphan spirit could not see what was available to them. In Jesus's three years of ministry on the earth He came to bring an astounding revelation. Jesus taught that the God of Israel—the God who had journeyed with the nation since its infancy, the God who had brought the nation out of slavery in Egypt, the God who created a nation and gave the people a name, and the God who saved them in countless battles—was, in fact, Abba Father, the

One Adam and Eve chose to abandon in the Garden of Eden.

After Jesus pointed people back to their Father, the question became, how do they return to the kingdom of God? How do people gain restoration of their rightful home and space? There is a debt to pay to come into right standing with God. There was a judgment levied against humanity that went all the way back to Adam and Eve for their abandonment of God. John 3:16 tells us the final verdict in the case was "for God so loved the world, that he gave his only begotten Son, that whosoever believeth in him should not perish, but have everlasting life." God loved His creation so much that He decided to pay the debt Himself by investing His Son into the earth. In Christ's death the debt for sins was paid, and the consequences of slavery and bondage to sin and death of purpose that plagued Adam, Eve, and their children were reversed. Jesus descended into hell and with all authority and power took back the key to humanity's identity that was snatched by the serpent in the Garden of Eden. If that were all Jesus did—paid our debt to sin and got back our identity from hell—this story would still have a powerful ending. However, Jesus did not stop at dying and plundering hell for three days. After He grabbed the keys to death, hell, and the grave, the Spirit of God resurrected Jesus from the dead! Why was it important for Him to be resurrected from the dead? With the resurrection God could shine the way back home to our rightful place as sons and daughters. God's plan all along was to restore us back to our rightful place as sons and daughters in the kingdom of God. Gaining victory over sin, death, and the grave as well as revealing our stolen identity is easy for God to do. What brings God joy is receiving us back into the kingdom of God as sons and daughters!

The plan God had all along worked. The promise of Genesis 3:15 manifested just as God said; His Son crushed the head of the serpent Satan in hell and took back that which was stolen in the garden—our identity as sons and daughters of Abba. God's plan worked through the death and resurrection of Jesus Christ. Thus, everyone who believes in Jesus as the final verdict declared in John 3:16 is now eligible to come back home to the kingdom of God as a son or daughter, free to spend time in the presence of the Father as we consistently communicate with and worship Him. We are now free to bask in the love of the Father, free to never have to leave the Father. Who would ever think to say no to this invitation of freedom to live as a son or daughter of Abba?

"I AM NOT A SLAVE MASTER"

Millions of people every day forfeit their invitation to freely live as Abba's sons and daughters. You may be wondering what life looks like for those who choose to do it apart from God's promise in Jesus Christ. It looks like a person who chooses to remain a slave to "the lust of the flesh,...the lust of the eyes, and the pride of life" (1 John 2:16). Verse 16 states, "For all that is in the world, the lust of the flesh, and the lust of the eyes, and the pride of life, is not of the Father, but is of the world." Living apart from Abba without embracing the revelation of Abba is an existence of destruction, snares, and temptation. "The lust of the flesh," or feeling the need to do something else to be satisfied, replaces the God-given identity as sons and daughters in those who have chosen to live apart from Abba. This lust can be for sex, drugs, food, money, or whatever fix an individual chooses to satisfy his physical needs with before spiritual needs. Some people will fill their identity with "the lust of the eyes," taking what seems to be the easy way in life—the shortcuts of cheating and lies—which only leads to destruction. Others fill their identity with "the pride of life," which causes them to jump into something without consulting God because after all, slaves are orphans, so they have no one who cares what they do or where they have been. These individuals fill their identity with a false sense of "I can handle it," while only drawing under the pressures of their circumstances and life decisions.

It is so easy to think, "These poor unbelieving slaves! If only they would receive Jesus Christ as their Lord and Savior." However, I want you to consider how many believers you know who still live under the pressure of their history. Maybe that person is you. These believers are individuals whose pasts still define how they live today because they cannot get past memories of what fathers did or did not do for them. I believe these individuals are living under the factors behind their "testimony," such as the feelings of guilt, shame, regret, and sadness over the past. The factors are the memories or emotions that they rehearse over and over again that keep them from moving beyond their past. These factors keep them under constant pressure to prove that they are no longer who they used to be. For others the pressure is to keep their history from being known for fear that they would be rejected if people knew who they really were. Instead they will live like lonely, rejected, alienated, and fearful orphans. These people live under the mantra "You don't know my story." This common anthem of many Christians is only code for "I am a slave to my past" because they are in chains bound to their history. They bought into the lie of the devil that their past is greater than God's work of redemption. When a person becomes a child of God, his history is not as significant as it once was because he has been purchased by God's investment of His Son.

History makes slaves, but so do circumstances, genetics, and experiences. There are different kinds of slaves in today's world. Some slaves only do heavy labor, and others are sex slaves. These individuals are captured and brought into slavery through various ways. Historically in the United States slaves were brought from Africa to work on plantations. They had limited movement and no right or freedom to explore beyond where they lived. Slaves worked under overbearing authority with no pay. They were relegated to a life of going to work, laboring, and having nothing to show for their work. They lived in constant fear of punishment because the plantation owners had the right to beat them if their work was perceived to have been completed incorrectly. Also slaves often did not have surnames. They did not have a family name because they were considered property of a franchise. They were simply identified by the plantation where they worked.

Even though the Emancipation Proclamation "freed" the slaves in the United States in 1863, we still live in a culture of slavery today. We just call it civilization, and it is the idea that we work unto nothing. We labor, we are beaten down by life circumstances, and we end life never really sharing a meaningful legacy. Our lives are identified by the plantation of our careers, accolades, or sins. Some people live like the woman with the issue of blood, who was a slave because of the stigma of her condition, which caused her to lose her name and only become known by her condition. (See Luke 8:43–48.) Others live like the blind man at the pool of Bethesda, who was known for his blindness. (See Mark 8:22–25.) In the same way, you are a man with an expensive car, a woman with a PhD, or a man who cheated on his wife. When we live our lives infirm, blind, deaf, lame, or dumb to the revelation of Abba as Father and His desire to give us new names as sons and daughters, we are nothing more than slaves. We also have people in our culture who willfully subject themselves to a life of slavery. They sentence themselves to slavery through unhealthy relationships and physical habits. Even individuals who live isolated and are unable to make friends are self-appointed slaves because slaves did not have rights and privileges to make friends or be in public.

There are even different kinds of slaves who are captured and brought into slavery various ways. In the same manner, Christians' lives are captured as well. I meet with people every day who want to be free in different areas of their lives. They try for a bit and want to believe that there is freedom for their sin, carnality, or care in the world, but then they lose hope that freedom is a possibility. Instead, they choose to live a captive life, thinking and acting like slaves. The devil tricks them into sin cycles and points the finger back to God, saying, "He is a slave master. If His standards were not so high, you would not keep doing, thinking, or feeling like this." However, God wants you to know He is not a slave master. The devil is behind your captivity. As a matter of fact, Abba makes a way out of captivity for you by giving you freedom in His Son, Jesus Christ.

A Liberating Father

Living a life of slavery to the cares of the world or fear, limited by our experiences, definitions, and conclusions, was never the plan of God for your life. God's plan all along was to liberate you. God's desire is not for you to live as a slave but to live through His identity as Abba, a liberating Father. Abba planned to liberate you through the spirit of adoption. In Romans 8:15 Paul notes, "For ye have not received the spirit of bondage again to fear; but ye have received the Spirit of adoption, whereby we cry, Abba, Father."

The spirit of adoption is perhaps the highest liberty God can provide for us; it gives us the freedom to become His sons and daughters. We literally have no limitations and nothing to fear, as Paul says in Romans 8:15, when Abba is the anchor of our lives as our Father. When our liberating Father adopts us back as sons and daughters, He leads both in the high and low moments of our lives. In the high moments of life we can shout, "Abba, our Father, has liberated us into peace and joy!" Paul says even at the lowest points of our lives we can cry, "Abba, our Father" in grief and sorrow, and God will be there to liberate us. Nothing is too hard for Abba to set us free. Nothing is too complicated for Abba to liberate us. Nothing is too simple or insignificant for Abba's liberating grace.

The spirit of adoption grants us the liberty to confidently declare our freedom from the cares of the world. The spirit of adoption leads us to our place in the kingdom of God as sons and daughters and gives us rest from the curse of laboring, toiling, labels, the captivity to our desires and emotions, and ultimately eternal death. Paul tells us that slavery and captivity to sin disqualified us as recipients of our intended positions in the kingdom of God as Abba's sons and daughters. In Romans 8:15 Paul reminds us that the judgments placed upon humanity in the Garden of Eden caused us to be disqualified as sons and daughters. At best the promise made in the garden extended to followers of God within the nation of Israel but not to outsiders such as us. However, because of God's liberating love for us as a Father, Jesus Christ was able to set the whole world into the freedom of being God's children. Through Christ's ministry, death, and resurrection everyone who believes in Him is freely grafted into the kingdom of God as Abba's sons and daughters. Because of Christ's offering for us on the cross Paul in Galatians 3:28 gives us a revelation of our liberating Father's hope and the motive of His heart: "There is neither Jew nor Greek, there is neither bond nor free, there is neither male nor female: for ye are all one in Christ Jesus." Through the Father's liberating grace we have been made into new people, into adopted sons and daughters of Abba.

Through the liberating move of the Father in Jesus Christ we were given a name and a right place. We were given the name of sons and daughters of Abba. We were set free from slavery to sin. We are no longer to be identified by our past. We are now free to be called by our rightful names as Abba's sons and daughters. Christ pointed us back to our rightful place. He connected humanity back to Abba's identity that He has been fulfilling since Old Testament times. Jesus revealed to us that God has been liberating and giving a name to those who otherwise would not have it throughout Israel's history. God liberated Enoch from death as he simply walked until he walked no more (Heb. 11:5). He liberated Noah and his family from the flood. God liberated Joseph from Potiphar's prison sentence. He liberated the people of Israel from four hundred years of slavery. He liberated the Israelites from their enemies and again from Babylonian captivity. Hosea 11:1 says, "When Israel was a child, then I loved him, and called my son out of Egypt." God is using language here to explain His attitudes and actions toward the nation of Israel. God desired to rescue the Israelites from their slave masters and give them a new name. He desired that people no longer be known as slaves; instead, He wanted them liberated to become a nation of His children because He loved them. It was the love of the liberating that set the Israelites free and gave them access to God's new name for them as a nation.

When Israel was under the reign of Egypt, the people were subjected to slavery under Pharaoh and to fear, curses, toiling, and a lack of identity in God and themselves. Yet when they cried to the Lord, Abba's liberating grace set them free. (See Exodus 5–14.) Hosea says it beautifully in the verse quoted previously. Even when the Israelites were immature in their juvenile stage, when they were controlled by or held in custodianship by their oppressors, God loved them. He loved them enough to set them free and give them a new name as a nation. That is so powerful because seldom do people believe that God loves them in the midst of oppression or while they are under the weight, hold, or grip of sin. People end up feeling that God loves them only because He wants them out of a particular situation or sin. However, as Hosea 11:1 states, while the Israelites were in bondage and in slavery, God loved them. For those who feel they need to clean themselves before they come to God or fully believe the revelation that God is our liberating Father, what Paul says in Romans 8:15 gives an invitation. Abba invites us to cry to Him and to call out to Him as Father in our immature state and whatever slave situation we are in today. Abba invites us to cry out to Him, and He will come to set us free. Abba will help you wherever or whenever you need Him because He is a liberating Father. Abba's invitation to be our Father who liberates is all-encompassing. Not only will He set us free; the Bible says our Father will also hide us to never be found again by the kingdom from which we escaped and from where we were purchased. In times of trouble and in times of plenty Abba invites us to receive His identity as our Father who liberates us, hides us in His love, and adopts us as His sons and daughters.

PURSUE FREEDOM IN SONSHIP

Abba's invitation to liberate us and adopt us as sons and daughters is an invitation to sonship. We are to embrace Abba's identity as a liberating Father by pursuing sonship, which is the nature of Jesus Christ. Sonship is how we live in such close relationship with the Father that everything about us changes into the likeness of the Father. The invitation to become sons and daughters of Abba is entered into through relationship with Jesus Christ. When we received Jesus Christ as our Lord and Savior, God immediately invited us to sonship. Abba's heart is to liberate us and give us new names as sons and daughters. In exchange our hearts must be to pursue our Father's heart and seek sonship. When we take on the essence of sonship, we enter into the relationship of Jesus Christ with Abba. In sonship we enter into the dynamics, conversations, and complexities of Jesus's relationship with Abba. Through the spirit of adoption in Jesus Christ sonship allows us to be not only engrafted into benefits of Jesus Christ's salvation and deliverance but also integrated into the tone and tenor of Jesus's relationship with Abba.

Therefore, as we see Jesus interacting with Abba and pursuing sonship, we too must pursue the freedom God grants us in sonship. Paul goes on in Romans 8:29 to share that "for whom he did foreknow, he also did predestinate to be conformed to the image of his Son, that he might be the firstborn among many brethren." This means that once we receive God as Abba and He adopts us, His plan is to help us become like His Son. Abba's desire is for us to pursue freedom in Him by being conformed to or integrated into the tone and tenor of His relationship with Jesus. We must pursue the freedom of sonship in our hearts, our minds, and our habits. As we relate to Abba as His sons and daughters, we will experience a heart transformation, a renewing of our minds, and an alteration in our habits that will empower us to live in sonship with our Father.

Heart transformation

Sonship starts with the transformation of our hearts. Transformation begins here for Abba's sons and daughters because the heart is the base, or headquarters, of not only our natural lives but also our spiritual lives. In the natural your heart is the headquarters of your whole body. It pumps blood throughout your body, which provides it with oxygen and nutrients. The heart also helps carry waste out of your body, and without that you could not live. Similarly the heart is the basis for our spiritual lives. Jesus said, "But those things which proceed out of the mouth come forth from the heart; and they defile the man. For out of the heart proceed evil thoughts, murders, adulteries, fornications, thefts, false witness, blasphemies" (Matt. 15:18–19). The heart is the headquarters for our beliefs and motives and even ultimately our actions. When we purpose in our hearts to believe God's identity as Abba, our liberating Father, He first begins to work on our hearts so our beliefs and motives, and then our actions, can be transformed into those of Christ, the perfect Son. Abba desires that our hearts be transformed into hearts that mirror Jesus's. He wants to transform our hearts from hearts of stone to hearts of flesh. It is also a transformation from orphan hearts to the hearts of sons and daughters.

The sin nature made Adam's and Eve's hearts grow cold and become like stone toward God. We know this because Genesis 3:8 records that after they ate the fruit, Adam's and Eve's inclination when they heard God was to run and abandon their Father. They were tricked by Satan to believe that Abba was a slave master who had strict rules, which fostered their desire to eat the fruit of the forbidden tree. Adam and Eve no longer saw God as Father, and it motivated them to eat of the forbidden tree and ultimately changed their habits. Prior to their fall into sin their habit was to run into the arms of Abba Father when He came into the garden, but after their fall they were running away. Their hearts had completely changed, turning away from God. They grew cold and had no love for the Father. This is the heart we all have before we come to know God as Abba Father. It is a heart of stone that nurtures our own desires, is motivated by our own passions, and is moving in the opposite direction of God. Despite the heart of stone that causes us to hate God, God made a promise: "A new heart also will I give you, and a new spirit will I put within you: and I will take away the stony heart out of your flesh, and I will give you an heart of flesh" (Ezek. 36:26). Abba makes good on this promise through Jesus Christ! As we live in relationship with Jesus and pursue Abba our Father's liberating love as His sons and daughters, He takes our cold hearts bent on doing as we please and transforms them into hearts of flesh. The day we receive Jesus in our hearts as our Lord and Savior we receive brand-new hearts, just as Abba promised! As we continue to pursue sonship, we will begin to learn how to steward our new hearts. This is why salvation is not the end point of our lives but the beginning. Our pursuit of Abba, our liberating Father, frees us to be custodians of the tone and tenor of Jesus's relationship with Abba. The lifelong journey of sonship transforms our beliefs, motives, and actions for the rest of our lives to align with those of our Father as He relates to Jesus.

The pursuit of Abba's liberating grace in sonship also transforms our hearts from orphan hearts to the hearts of sons and daughters. The sin that caused Adam and Eve to abandon God also created anxiety, fear, and panic. They were anxious about what God would say to them, and they were fearful of what He would do, so they panicked and ran from God. The same bondages of the orphans that Adam and Eve chose to become in the Garden of Eden plague us even to this day. The orphan heart is a heart filled with anxiety about decision-making, fear over the future, and panic about being transparent. The orphan heart is a sentence to a life of condemnation, where those who have it are irrationally hard on themselves because they are anxious and fearful and in constant panic. When we come into relationship with Jesus Christ as our Lord and Savior, Abba's love liberates us from the bondages of sin that gave us orphan hearts and transforms us back to our rightful place as sons and daughters with hearts like Jesus's. Unfortunately, because most Christians do not believe in the fullness of God's identity as Abba our Father, they do not pursue Abba's freedom in sonship and instead continue exhibiting the behaviors of orphan hearts. For those who accept the invitation from the Father to receive Him as Abba, their lifelong pursuit of Abba's freedom in sonship helps transform their old emotions of anxiety, fear, and panic that were inherent in their orphan hearts to the hearts of sons and daughters filled with peace, boldness, and joy.

Renewing of the mind

On the pursuit of Abba's liberating call to sonship our heart transformation leads to a renewing of our minds as well. God is a liberating Father who desires for us, His sons and daughters, to enjoy the same benefits Jesus does. Jesus's benefit as a son was that He had freedom in His thoughts and inner fears because His heart was that of a child of God. Jesus never doubted Abba's identity, abilities, or capabilities, nor did He ever doubt Himself. The pursuit of sonship in Abba allowed Jesus to be fully secure in His beliefs, motives, and actions. Sons and daughters of Abba today have the ability to access the same peace of mind and heart that Jesus had throughout His lifetime on the earth. Romans 12:2 urges us, "Do not conform to the pattern of this world, but be transformed by the renewing of your mind. Then you will be able to test and approve what God's will is—his good, pleasing and perfect will" (NIV). Through the pursuit of the freedom Abba grants us in sonship, the transformation of our hearts will begin to require our minds to be renewed in the Word of God. The renewing of our minds happens as we divorce the past and rehearse the Word of God.

Renewing our minds in the Word of God helps fortify our new hearts as sons and daughters of Abba and teaches us the ways of sonship in the kingdom of God versus the kingdom of darkness. Sons and daughters must pursue the freedom of relationship with Abba by confessing the Word of God because it helps us to live out the beliefs, motives, and actions of what was established in Jesus and Abba's relationship. The beginning of our journey to renewing our minds will be very uncomfortable because our hearts have to get used to the freedom of sonship. However, it will be a journey worth every step as we live securely in the truth of Abba's identity and the reality of His call for us to be sons and daughters.

We start the journey of renewing our minds by committing in our hearts to hate the very thing that oppressed us. It may be odd, but it is not always common for people to hate their oppressors. Remember when Moses led the Israelites out of Egypt? The people started to complain that at least their oppressors were consistent. "When we were in Egypt, we had leeks, we had onions, and we knew where our provision was coming from" is what they told Moses (author's paraphrase; see Numbers 11:1–15). They complained to Moses that they did not know what this God wanted from them and why their journey was taking so long. Under Pharaoh the people of Israel were programmed as slaves to live with constant thoughts of hopelessness and fear. They were fearful, fear led, and fear driven. Their inability to live as children of God caused them to have no peace. They longed for the slavery of the past because slavery and fear provided their frame of reference. The same thing will and does happen to some of Abba's sons and daughters today, those who do not renew their minds in the Word of Abba. We become sons and daughters who still live with orphan hearts because we have not fully committed to hating the thoughts and fears of sin and the beliefs, motives, and actions to which sin leads us.

Our pursuit of Abba's freedom of sonship requires us to rehearse the Word of Abba consistently to renew our minds. Philippians 2:5 says, "Let this mind be in you, which was also in Christ Jesus." Reciting the Word of God is important for Abba's sons and daughters because it allows our minds to be renewed into the mind-set of Jesus. The renewing of our minds transforms the thoughts that emerge from our hearts. Our transformed hearts as sons and daughters will have the thoughts of God versus the old thoughts of slavery from the orphan hearts. The renewing of the mind in the Word of God is literally a reprogramming of our minds from the old slavery mind-set of sin to the mind of Christ in Abba.

As Abba's children we must spend time meditating on, reciting, and studying the Word of God, believing and declaring our Father's promises over our lives. Whenever someone hears a promise of Abba and thinks, "I can't have that because I have done something to make me undeserving," it is a direct manifestation of slavery. When an individual hears the revelation of Abba and chooses not to believe that Abba wants to freely give and help him as a son to walk in the revelation of God, his mind needs to be renewed. As sons and daughters we need to meditate on Scripture, recite it daily, and research the Word of God. We can study the Father's love for us according to His Word. Our meditation, recitation, and study will help hide Abba's Word in our newly transformed hearts of sonship. We can study things such as Abba's compassion for us, His dislikes, and His motives. This way when old thoughts of slavery or fear arise, we are empowered to combat them with the truth of Abba's Word. In the pursuit of Abba's freedom in sonship, pursue becoming a lover of the Word of God, and your mind will be renewed to live fully in sonship.

Altered habits

Transformed hearts and renewed minds in pursuit of Abba's freedom in sonship ultimately lead to the alteration of our habits, or our actions and reactions. Remember, Romans 12:2 says, "Do not conform to the pattern of this world, but be transformed by the renewing of your mind. Then you will be able to test and approve what God's will is—his good, pleasing and perfect will" (NIV). When our hearts are transformed to believe Abba Father, our minds can be renewed and our thoughts are no longer those of anxiety, fear, and panic, as Adam and Eve experienced in the Garden of Eden. Transformed hearts of sonship live fully in the "good, pleasing and perfect" thoughts of Abba found in His Word. We no longer operate out of a place of fear and panic. Instead, we act upon God's Word. Our hearts are at peace and calm with the directives of Abba recorded in the Bible, so our actions are bold and secure. Jesus was the perfect example of how we are to live as Abba's children, with altered habits. In Abba's freedom of sonship we do as He does. John 5:19 states, "Then answered Jesus and said unto them, Verily, verily, I say unto you, The Son can do nothing of himself, but what he seeth the Father do: for what things soever he doeth, these also doeth the Son likewise." Jesus's complete pursuit of sonship in the Father resulted in His seeing and doing only what He saw the Father see and do.

Our pursuit of sonship will naturally alter our habits. Our habits, or our actions and reactions to situations and circumstances in life, are the sum total of what our hearts and our minds see and do. Our habits reveal the sum total of our minds and hearts' activities. Therefore if our habits are lacking in boldness and filled with anxiety or fear of the future, then we are not living in the fullness of sonship as Abba's sons and daughters. The pursuit of sonship with Abba gives us a freedom that brings peace and security to our actions. When we allow Abba to give us the freedom of sonship in our hearts and our minds, then our sight and actions align with our Father. Our transformed hearts and renewed minds will naturally lead to our seeing Abba, ourselves, and others as He intended. Instead of our eyes seeing a slave master, our bondage, and the devastation of slavery among others, Abba gives us the reality of what He sees when He sees us. Our habit of sitting and looking at life from a place of defeat changes to an elevated place of sonship when we pursue sonship in Abba. Our hearts and minds are altered to habitually dwell from our rightful place as Abba's sons and daughters seated in heavenly places with our Father who react to situations and circumstances directly from Abba's vantage point and not our own desires and plans.

The change of habits we experience in sonship with Abba is long-lasting because it is led by the right motives and rooted in the truth of the Word of God. When we pursue sonship, Abba is going to change what we work toward, what we work for, what we believe will reward us, and how far we are willing to go. Our sonship in Abba will cause our actions to mirror those of Jesus so we too can dwell in the complete and total freedom of Christ.

We Are Finishers

Abba's invitation to sonship grants us the freedom to live under His identity as our liberating Father. When we are freed from the bonds of slavery, we have the freedom to receive not only Abba's identity but also our identity. Our pursuit of sonship in Abba ultimately reveals who our Father has called us to be. When we pursue a relationship of sonship with our Father, we find fortitude of our purpose. Sonship is the strength of our identity. In sonship we find and strengthen our mission in life and have the right hearts, minds, and habits to live completely in the fullness of who Abba has designed us to be. Our sonship gives us free access to fulfill our callings, utilize our gifts to the glory of Abba, and accomplish our purpose.

There is an issue when people pursue callings, gifts, and purpose without being rooted in sonship. If sonship is the strength, or fuel, of our purpose, then apart from sonship we have nothing to fuel our gifts, callings, and purpose. This is why so many people run out of gas on the way to living their God-given callings, gifts, and purpose. They end up running out of gas because they are pursuing callings, gifts, and purpose with orphan hearts rather than hearts of sons and daughters of Abba.

Remember that those with orphan hearts live with an orphan identity in which they are slaves. They are self-punishing, self-abusing, and pessimistic captives who view themselves, Abba, and others with suspicion and distrust. Those with orphan hearts also live out of an identity of rebellion, in which they are in pursuit of their own desires and plans for life. Where there are orphan hearts in operation in our identity, there is bound to be disobedience as we pursue our callings, gifts, anointing, purpose, and desires over God's will. When those with orphan hearts choose to live in disobedience, they choose slavery over their identity of sonship. Those with disobedient orphan hearts are plagued with an identity filled with insecurity. They live in consistent hesitation, anxiety, and fear, and in a panic over what Abba instructs, advises, and admonishes them to accomplish.

Those who do not fully embrace Abba's identity as a liberating Father and are without His liberating grace often live with cycles of sin, cycles of starting something new, and even cycles of trauma. They are likely slaves to their flesh or the fleshly actions of others. They may be lonely because they are afraid of loving others. When there is a fear of purely giving or receiving love, there is an orphan identity at work. The biggest sign of an orphan identity is the inability to complete anything. Those with an orphan identity typically have a hard time finishing a project, a book, or a business and ultimately cannot finish their life calling, mission, identity, or purpose. The orphan heart cannot finish anything because it is a slave to everything else the world offers. It is a slave to the characteristics of sin, condemnation, and anxiety.

The identity of a son or a daughter, on the other hand, is a finisher. We are finishers because Abba's Son was a finisher. Jesus was able to complete His mission and fully live in the complete identity of sonship. Therefore as we pursue sonship with Abba, we receive the strength to finish all that Abba has purposed for us to accomplish. We are not working out of our own strength; we are working out of the completed work of Jesus Christ on the cross. In contrast, those living with an orphan identity as slaves cannot finish anything because sin lost the battle at Jesus's death and resurrection. Therefore those with an orphan identity will always feel as if they are at a disadvantage or that they cannot win. The victory of the finishing move is found in Jesus's total and complete victory. The ability to finish victoriously is freely given by Abba to those who receive the revelation of Him as Abba.

Sons and daughters of Abba are also finishers because their beliefs, motives, and actions are aligned with the tone and tenor of Abba through Jesus Christ. Sonship freely gives us transformed hearts that first love Abba as His children. As Abba's children we accomplish the mission, calling, and purpose to which Abba has called us because our hearts are to please our Father. We finish as an act of love to demonstrate to our Father how much we appreciate His anointing, skills, and gifts in our lives. Sonship solidifies our identity as finishers because we have the minds to accomplish whatever God has called us to complete. Thoughts of fear or failure do not bind us because when we receive Abba's invitation to freely pursue sonship through the meditation, recitation, and study of the Word of God, we are filled with the truth of Abba. And the truth of God's Word can help us fight against whatever thought or fear seeks to come against our finishing or fulfilling what Abba has called us to complete.

In addition, as Abba's sons and daughters we also freely live in the identity of finishers because our actions and habits are not our own. Sonship calls us to freely see and do what Abba sees and does concerning a person, a situation, or circumstances. We are not groping around in the dark. We have clear vision from our vantage point next to our Father, and we have access to clear and specific directives on how to accomplish our gifts, callings, and purpose because we can ask Abba directly in prayer. We finish because we have free access to the Father's wisdom. We finish because if we ask Abba, He will give us the steps, processes, and solutions we need to finish. David put it best when he said, "For the LORD God is a sun and shield: the LORD will give grace and glory: no good thing will he withhold from them that walk uprightly" (Ps. 84:11). We, Abba's children, are finishers because Abba will not withhold any good thing from us. He will freely liberate us into victory through His Son. We do not have to waste time trying our own plans and purposes in life. We do not have to waste time in trial and error. We do not have to waste time feeling worn out. In a relationship with Abba, our liberating Father, we have the freedom to give up the habits of slaves and live in the freedom of our identity as finishers, as sons and daughters fully led by Abba.

4

OUR INSEPARABLE FATHER

Abba Is Not Distant

*That they all may be one; as thou, Father, art in me,
and I in thee, that they also may be one in us: that
the world may believe that thou hast sent me.*

∞∞∞ JOHN 17:21 ∞∞∞

JESUS USED PRAYER to reveal Abba Father to us. The Gospel of John offers one of the few records of Jesus's personal prayers between Himself and the Father in chapter 17. It records Jesus's beloved disciple John overhearing Jesus praying and gives us access to the types of things Jesus communicated with Abba. Jesus prays: "I pray for them: I pray not for the world, but for them which thou hast given me; for they are thine. And all mine are thine, and thine are mine; and I am glorified in them" (John 17:9–10). This part of the prayer is the beginning of a concept we find throughout the New Testament: we are all part of God's creation, but we are not all God's sons and daughters.

The idea that we are all God's children is one of the primary lies about God's identity in our culture. It is centered on the idea that a person can live however he chooses, and as long as he is a "good" person or performs good deeds, he can claim God in eternity. But Abba Father is not interested in members of some social club, where admission is based on personal merit. God is looking for sons and daughters to share an inheritance with Jesus. Belonging to God, then, does not happen by virtue of our existence. Belonging happens when we respond to what Jesus did to facilitate our adoption into the family of God.

The popular yet false notion is that because God is the idea, brains, and genius behind creation, all human beings are automatically His children. The sole driving force behind this notion is Satan, who has been working this plan since the beginning of creation, starting with Adam and Eve and continuing to today, to cause humanity to be separated from God's truth. His goal has been to trick us into thinking we can do anything that we want to do because, as long as we do some good, this abstract higher power will not have a problem with it. According to this logic you do not need to have a relationship with God. This lie is geared at keeping us separated from the person of God and out of Abba's presence, which causes us to lack knowledge of the power and identity God promises His sons and daughters. Paul says in Ephesians 2:19 that before we came into the kingdom of God through Jesus Christ to receive God as Abba, we were strangers, foreigners, and citizens of darkness. Jesus said we belonged to a father, who is the devil (John 8:44). We are not all God's children—not until we receive Jesus Christ as our Lord and Savior. We are living separated from God and blind to it because of Satan's lies.

For this reason Jesus was purposeful in revealing God as Abba to us, and He spent time during His earthly ministry praying and making intercession for us—something He continues to do today. Our journey from darkness to light involves an exchange in who gets to parent us. We leave behind Satan, who parented us into destructive patterns of sin, and enter into a new relationship with Abba Father, who parents us into life-giving sonship. We need to learn that God is Abba so we can be open to making the divine exchange from a life of sin to the more of God as Abba's child. Otherwise we are nothing more than individuals in God's creation who have chosen not to become Abba's children and instead have chosen to live a life of sin apart from God.

SEPARATED

Sin has serious effects on a person's life. One of the things that grieves me as a prophet is how comfortable with and tolerant of sin believers are. I am grieved for those who are unwilling to radically get rid of, lose, or forgo relationships that promote sin, sin cycles, and sin behaviors. They rationalize sin tolerance with the misapplication of Romans 3:23: "For all have sinned, and come short of the glory of God." They determine to come out of sin in the way they are most comfortable, which typically translates to a refusal to let go of certain friendships or a refusal to stop fornicating, stop watching porn, or come out of agreement with addictions or whatever sin their vice is. They don't understand that sin is the program and strategy of Satan to separate them from Abba so he can destroy and murder them.

Jesus said, as recorded in John 8:44, "Ye are of your father the devil, and the lusts of your father ye will do. He was a murderer from the beginning, and abode not in the truth, because there is no truth in him. When he speaketh a lie, he speaketh of his own: for he is a liar, and the father of it." Jesus explains to us here that the strategy of Satan is to program sin into our nature—our habits, desires, and decisions. Sin is designed to rob us of the knowledge of Abba's deep love for us and our identity as His sons and daughters. Sin ultimately destroys the quality of our lives. Satan has a customized plan for each of us. All of us have at one point cooperated with this plan, and many still do. Some are unaware it is even at work in their lives. Whatever your vice happens to be, it is a plan tailor-made by Satan with two objectives: to separate you from Abba so Satan can kill your purpose, and to separate you from Abba so Satan can destroy your identity as His son or daughter.

Sin attacks our purpose and the reason we were born. Satan accomplishes this by encouraging us to chase after our own human desires. As humans when we choose our own will over the plans of God, we participate in sin by choosing to live separate from Abba. The prophet Isaiah told us in Isaiah 59:2, "But your iniquities have separated between you and your God, and your sins have hid his face from you, that he will not hear." When we separate from God, we lose our purpose, which is to be

Abba's son or daughter. When our purpose as sons and daughters is destroyed, then all the blessings of identity that come with sonship are destroyed, which brings us to the other goal of sin. Blessings such as living like beloved children of Abba or being known as finishers are unavailable to us because we are disconnected from Abba, who is the source of our identity. That's why sin is so dangerous; it separates us from God. Sin separates us from our rightful purpose to be Abba's child and our identity of sonship.

It's no wonder Jesus prayed for us in John 17. We are in an all-out war. Satan is working hard to keep us separated from our Father by seducing us with sin. Sin is like a seductive mistress. We have to treat it as we would a home-wrecker and refuse to give it access to our lives! How sin manifests will differ from person to person. What tempts one person to sin may not be her neighbor's temptation. However, the ultimate vision of Satan for sin and its activity in our lives is always the same: to keep us from drawing close to Abba so we will abandon our purpose as sons and daughters of Abba and live in an identity crisis for the rest of our lives.

Jesus prayed for us because He knew that Abba's desire was not to live separate from us. God is committed to living inseparable from us. He wants us to draw so close to Him that His identity becomes our own. Abba is so dedicated to living in intimacy with us that He sent His Son, Jesus Christ, to die for our sins. Through Christ's death and resurrection and Abba's mercy and grace, Satan's plan to keep us separated from God was defeated.

"I AM NOT DISTANT"

God loves His creation and desires for us all to choose to be in close relationship with Him. While nothing can separate us from the love of God, the objective of Satan for humanity, for both Christians and non-Christians, is to make it seem as if God is distant from us. As I stated, the primary tool Satan uses is sin, with the goal being to keep us from living with Abba as our Father so we do not experience our God-given purpose of sonship and Abba's revelation of our identity. When we do not know our purpose or identity, we feel separated from God and divided in our allegiance between God and sin. When we are divided in our allegiance, we ultimately lack purpose, identity, and power to destroy Satan's works in our lives. The work of sin in our lives manifests through fear, failure, abandonment, and hell. When these things are in operation in our lives, Satan uses them as tactics to distance us from God here on the earth and for eternity.

Fear

Fear chases us away from God's presence and makes it seem as if Abba is distant from us. Instead of leaning on Abba, we are separated from Him. Fear is a magnifier, and the magnification of a problem, circumstance, or person causes us to conclude that there is something between us and God that is not only bigger than us but also bigger than God. It seems big enough to make God distant and unable to rescue us. Instead of seeking Abba in moments of fear, we are led into the sin of rebellion by seeking our own solutions. We choose to do what we want to do, which is nothing at all or the opposite of

Abba's will because we must save ourselves, as He is distant. Fear is a trap to give us the wrong lens through which to see God, to make us see God as small and distant. However, God is not distant. Deuteronomy 31:6 reads: "Be strong and of a good courage, fear not, nor be afraid of them: for the LORD thy God, he it is that doth go with thee; he will not fail thee, nor forsake thee." Abba wants us to be courageous and to know that He is nearby and has not left us. Whatever our fears are, they are not bigger than Abba. Our situations or circumstances do not have the power to push God away. Abba can succeed and transcend anything that causes fear in our lives.

Failure

Satan also uses failure as a device to separate us from Abba Father, making us feel He is distant from us. Satan tries to shape our perception of failure as being a part of our identity rather than an event we can recover from with God. This is why we often hear people say, "I am a failure," or "I am afraid of being a failure." Satan often builds a case for fear of failure with evidence from the past. Often our ideas of God's distancing Himself from us because of our failures are rooted in what our natural parents or parental figures did with our victories and defeats as a child. If your parents only celebrated you and wanted to be close to you when you won, performed well, or behaved in whatever manner they thought was acceptable, then your definition of closeness is likely dependent on being perfect. This is impossible because you are a human being, and human beings are imperfect. Likewise most parental figures yell at, punish, or ground their children when they come home with low marks on a report card or test, when they do not behave correctly, or when they do not win. Thus, when you feel as if you have failed, you probably expect God to distance Himself and want nothing to do with you, just as you experienced in the past.

Imagine an unmarried person who has committed to a lifestyle of celibacy. After years of maintaining this commitment, he finds himself in a compromising position and gives in to temptation. Guilt and shame associated with the thoughts of failure may drive this individual away from the presence of God. Satan uses these moments to push the idea that God has distanced Himself from us when we make mistakes. Satan tells us this one failure signals our inability to be successful in our pursuit of wholeness and purity.

Satan's hope through these lies is to supplant our desire for change and lead us into hopelessness, saying things such as: "Why do I even try? I am such a failure! God must hate me now, so I might as well just stay away from Him." Coming into agreement with guilt and shame causes us to view God as distant. When Satan's lies go unchallenged in our minds and hearts, we begin to see God as separated from us. Because of this many people choose to distance themselves from God's presence, which was Satan's strategy all along. In times of failure we must remember that God is not distant. He is a loving Father who desires to be close to us and is willing to restore us and give us the power to destroy the works of Satan. Abba Father wants us to live as sons and daughters who do not fear failure but use moments when we've failed as opportunities to draw even closer to Him.

Paul wrote, "There is therefore now no condemnation to them which are in Christ Jesus, who walk not after the flesh, but after the Spirit" (Rom. 8:1). Abba wants you to know He is not distant, far off, or standing in judgment of you. He is your Father! You can never fail your Father. When you fail, it does not change your DNA, your last name does not change, and it does not change your outcome or your future in God. A failure is an event and not a destination. Abba is all-knowing, all-seeing, and all-perceiving, and despite your sin or failure He still desires to be your Father, if you are willing.

Abandonment

Feelings of abandonment can also lead us to conclude that God is distant. We may experience abandonment when we see unanswered prayer or during times of hardship. Sometimes when we pray, when we call out to God, or even when we read our Bibles, it can feel as if God is not there. In those moments we can feel as if God is distant. This often leads us to believe we did something to drive God away. Feeling forsaken is a normal response for a person met with hardship and difficulty. Even Jesus felt forsaken in the most difficult moment of His life as He hung from the cross. In Matthew 27:46 the Scriptures say, "And about the ninth hour Jesus cried with a loud voice, saying, Eli, Eli, lama sabachthani? That is to say, My God, my God, why hast thou forsaken me?" It is human to feel alone in the midst of struggle. The temptation in those moments is to believe that God is distant and withdrawn. Satan lies to us and actively convinces us that everyone, including God, has abandoned us. Actually the opposite is true. Abba wants us to know that He will not abandon us in our trials, and a lack of prayers answered as we would like is no reason to think He is distant. Natural fathers often forsake their children, friends can be flaky, and spouses sometimes forget their vows, but Abba will never abandon us. God has never distanced Himself from us. As a matter of fact, Jesus's cry on the cross gives us a strategy for handling times when we feel abandoned and distant from God. Jesus cried out to His Father because He knew Abba was not too far away. Acts 17:27 says, "That they should seek the Lord, if haply they might feel after him, and find him, though he be not far from every one of us." Jesus shows us that Abba wants to bring us closer to Him, and He is never too far away from any one of us.

Hell

The ultimate separation move for Satan is to cause us to live in the eternal torment of hell. I believe the torment of hell is caused by an eternity in total separation from God rather than by fires or flames. Hell is torment because God is not there and cannot be reached. It is a place of permanent separation from God. God never intended humans to go to hell; He created it for beings He did not want to be bothered with anymore. However, when humans chose to worship the beings God did not want to be bothered with, the only other place for these individuals to go was to the same location as what they worshipped. The individuals in hell are there based solely on the fact that they chose Satan's false identity for their lives over Abba's identity. They chose instead to partner with the devil, with the father of lies.

God wants you to know that eternal separation from Him was never His plan for His creation. Hell was never the intended destination for human beings, nor was it created to be our punishment. Ultimately God despises separation. The only one God wanted to be separate from was His enemy, Satan. Father God wants you to know that He is not your enemy, nor has He ever considered you His enemy. Abba does not want to live apart from you now or ever. Abba wants you to not see Him as distant but to know the truth that He is closer than you can ever imagine.

AN INSEPARABLE FATHER

Jesus's prayer in the Book of John reveals to us the truth of Abba's identity. John 17:21–22 records Jesus praying, and He asked God, "That they all may be one; as thou, Father, art in me, and I in thee, that they also may be one in us: that the world may believe that thou hast sent me. And the glory which thou gavest me I have given them; that they may be one, even as we are one." Jesus's prayer demonstrates that Abba's desire is to be one with us, to be inseparable from us. Abba desires to be our inseparable Father. Jesus's prayer was for God to be found in us and for us to be found in God. When we believe and receive the revelation of God as Abba, our inseparable Father, we will adequately see what we are capable of accomplishing and can live as Abba's sons and daughters in our identity of sonship. When we receive Abba's identity as inseparable, then the devil's plan to keep us in sin and seeing God as distant will not prosper. You must understand that Abba is inseparable from you, which means He is consistent and committed to being close to you at all times.

Consistent

We do not have many examples of consistency in our society today. There aren't many who are unchanging in their nature or who are close to us 24/7. Even if you have a great spouse, awesome friends, or good parents, the pressure of being present, unwavering, and unfluctuating is exhausting and impossible for human beings. People are not perfect; only God is. Abba, our inseparable Father, is unwavering and unchanging. Abba desires to be there for you 24/7.

As an inseparable Father, Abba is consistently unwavering, consistently steady, and consistently resolved in His love for us. Abba does not decide to love us one day and then push us away the next because of something we said or did. Psalm 102:27 says concerning Abba, "But thou art the same, and thy years shall have no end." God's love for us will not end. When we fail, sin, or feel abandoned or afraid, God does not distance Himself from us. In fact, He wants to draw even closer to us to restore us back to our rightful place as His sons and daughters. Often we are the ones who run from God in times of sin, fear, failure, or abandonment. We are the only ones who can separate us from Abba, and we do so by buying into Satan's lies against God.

Malachi 3:6 records God speaking to the people: "For I am the LORD, I change not; therefore ye sons of Jacob are not consumed." In a relationship with Abba through Jesus Christ we can be confident that Abba is consistently the same God He has always been. He is always protecting us, providing for us, and being there for us. Scripture says in that verse in Malachi that Abba does not change, which allows us to not be consumed by sin and the cares of the world. The unchanging consistency of Abba is what keeps us. Abba is so constant that through Jesus Christ He made it possible for us to live with Him now and in heaven for eternity.

Committed

Our inseparable Father is not just consistent. He is also committed to us. Abba is wholly dedicated and loyal to us. He established this truth by sending His Son, Jesus Christ, to the earth to die for our sins. Jesus's life, ministry, death, and resurrection were a sign that God was committed to being our inseparable Abba. Our Father was willing to make an investment in us before we were born. Before we ever made the decision to receive Jesus as our Lord and Savior, Abba was willing to show His commitment and desire to never be separated from us. If Jesus was all God did for us, it would certainly be more than enough to prove His commitment to be inseparable from us. In answer to Jesus's prayer, which we read in John 17:21–22, the Father took it one step further: He sent the Holy Spirit.

When Jesus was preparing to complete His earthly mission, His disciples were troubled at the thought of life without Him. Once, when Jesus announced He was going to leave them, Peter rebuked Jesus because he did not want to be separated from Him (Matt. 16:22). However, Jesus encouraged His disciples not to let their hearts be troubled at the thought of Him leaving (John 14:27). Jesus began to tell His disciples it was good for

Him to go away (in death and resurrection) because God was sending them the Holy Spirit (John 16:7). In Jesus's human form only those near Him had access. But with the coming of the Holy Spirit everyone who believed in Jesus could have access to the presence of God.

Jesus promised the Holy Spirit would be a helper, an advocate, a comforter, a counselor, a redeemer, and the Spirit of truth. Jesus assured the disciples that "I will not leave you as orphans; I will come to you" (John 14:18, NIV). Abba would never leave His sons and daughters alone, separated from Him. Jesus prayed for us to be one with God because He knew the Father wants to be inseparable from us. Abba Father answered Jesus's prayer in John 17:21–22 and showed His unrelenting commitment to being inseparable from us by sending the Holy Spirit to live on the inside of every one of us who comes to receive Him as Abba through Jesus. The Holy Spirit allows God to be within us and for us to be found within God, just as Jesus prayed.

In Ephesians 1:13–14 Paul tells us that the promised Holy Spirit is "a deposit guaranteeing our inheritance until the redemption of those who are God's possession" (NIV). The Holy Spirit is a guarantee of Abba's commitment to us. Abba is so committed to being our inseparable Father that He gave us His presence. Therefore anytime we need instruction, guidance, comfort, revelation, strength, or wisdom, we always have access to God. If we really believed this revelation, then sin would not be an issue for believers because every time our hearts would want to lead us to sin, we would immediately call on the Holy Spirit for help, guidance, and strength against temptation. If we truly believed Abba is committed to being inseparable from us, failure would not be an option because we would rely on the Holy Spirit, who is the Spirit of wisdom and truth. We would not need to make mistakes because the Holy Spirit would always give us the right answers in our decision making. We would never again think He has abandoned us because we would know Abba is closer than our breath. We would have peace from the Comforter to know that Abba is present within us, ready to attend to us so we would never have to fear being abandoned or distant from God. This is because Abba's commitment to us through the Holy Spirit is that He is never far away from us.

This commitment from Abba is why the baptism of the Holy Spirit in the Book of Acts is more than speaking in tongues. Speaking in tongues is great because it gives us a language in which to communicate directly with God, but the baptism of the Holy Spirit is also significant because the presence of God is now inseparable from us. The power, authority, wisdom, and guidance that Jesus had access to as a son of Abba is now accessible to all sons and daughters. At Pentecost He gave the whole of creation a right to be inseparable from the Father. Satan's plans to separate us from God were ruined. Humanity no longer needed to live as if they were orphans. In the Holy Spirit we have access to the Father all the time. If we have received Abba through Jesus Christ, we never have to feel distant or abandoned because our inseparable Father is always present, close, available, and consistently committed to being close to us.

PURSUE INTIMACY

Abba loves us and desires to never be apart from us. We must respond to Abba's desire to be inseparable from us by pursuing intimacy with Him. In our pursuit of intimacy we will have the power to do what Paul wrote in Galatians 5:16. We will live our lives by the Holy Spirit and not by our own desires. Our own desires may seem right to us, but they have the potential to lead us into sin, fear, failures, abandonment, and hell. Pursuing intimacy with our inseparable Father will cause us to die to our fleshly desires and live as one with God. We pursue intimacy with Abba through worship.

Some churches and individuals have studied worship, but as a whole the church does not understand worship. We support music departments at our churches and sing a few slow songs and call it worship. Human beings respond to melodies, so songs help us have a conversation with God. However, if our worship of Abba only consists of singing songs, we are not worshipping Him at all. The word *worship* in the Hebrew is *shachah*, which means "to bow in respect and reverence."[1] If our lives are not bowed to the Holy Spirit in complete respect and reverence for Abba, then it does not matter how many slow songs we sing to Him. One of the best quotes I have ever heard about worship comes from William Temple, the archbishop of Canterbury. He said:

> Worship is the submission of all of our nature to God. It is the quickening of conscience by His holiness; the nourishment of mind with His truth; the purifying of imagination by His beauty; the

opening of the heart to His love; the surrender of
will to His purpose—all this gathered up in adoration, the most selfless emotion of which our nature
is capable.[2]

To worship is to encounter God. It is encounters with
God that lead to holiness, truth, purity, love, purpose,
and surrender and fill us with adoration for Abba. Worship is encounters with God that help us bow to Him
and submit or surrender to being inseparable with the
holiness, truth, purity, love, and purpose of God.

Bow

We worship every single day of our lives. We either
worship God, or we worship our thoughts, our plans, and
our passions. Some people worship fear, anxiety, or their
past. Others worship their sin nature and desires. We find
many people today worshipping their sexual preferences
and relational dependencies. There are many people who
worship and intimately pursue earthly wisdom or careers
above God's wisdom. Whatever we choose to give our
total dependence to and whatever we see as greater than
ourselves we bow to in worship, believing it is greater
than ourselves. The things we bow to are what empower
us or enslave us. When we pursue intimacy with God by
bowing before Abba in worship, we are empowered to
live inseparable from Abba. If we intimately pursue anything else, we become slaves to that which we are worshipping and bowing to.

The interesting thing about bowing is that it is the
first thing we learn as babies, and we practice on our
mothers. Shortly after we were born, doctors likely

placed us on our mothers, even if just for a few seconds, so we could become acquainted with her. This helps babies become acquainted with the temperature, voice, rhythm, and feel of the ones who produced them. This is done because babies are not independent or mature. Babies are not self-confident and self-aware, and they do not have the ability to discern and differentiate. We start learning to bow at this moment because we must be subjected to a superior being who will teach us and protect us. This is necessary because babies need their parents to care for them and model important life skills, such as eating, walking, talking, and sharing with each other. God gives us this gift of learning to bow to our mothers as a protective mechanism so later in life, when we get to make a choice regarding whom to bow to, it is not too hard for us to choose to bow to Abba as our heavenly Father. Also, because of our experiences as infants, when we choose to worship Abba, we understand that living inseparably from Him means we must be completely dependent on His temperature, His voice, and His rhythm to teach us things such as maturity, confidence, self-awareness, and identity.

Even if we forget this first lesson nature taught us, the Bible has multiple passages that teach and train us on how to pursue intimacy with Abba and live as one with Him in worship. Hebrews 11:6 says, "But without faith it is impossible to please him: for he that cometh to God must believe that he is, and that he is a rewarder of them that diligently seek him." The first step to bowing before God is believing He is God and we are not. We must acknowledge that He is perfect and we are not, that He is the only living God and we are not, and that there is no need for Abba to share His glory, and we should not want to steal His glory. We must admit that we do not want to divide His authority with other things in our lives because He is sovereign. We must acknowledge that there is nothing in Abba that is a mistake. Once we acknowledge these truths, we cannot stop there; we must move on to the second step of worship, the most crucial step, and that is submission.

Submit

When we bow before the Father and come into agreement with the truth of Abba's identity, we become one with Him through submission. Submission is how we show our respect and reverence for Abba. We submit every time we choose Abba's will, His plans, His motives, and His thoughts over our own. If your pursuit of intimacy with Abba stops at simply acknowledging truths about Him, then you are not worshipping wholly, and you are not yet inseparable from Abba. To be inseparable, we must worship, and to worship, we must submit.

Most of us have a fear of submission. Abuse, control, corruption, manipulation, and bad upbringings have led to this fear. This has caused us to be skeptical and to mistrust whom and what we follow. After we learn to depend on our parents as children, we learn independence, submitting to no one. We hold to our emotions, ways of thinking, points of view, and desires because we have not yet met with someone we deem greater than ourselves. However, when Jesus Christ becomes our Lord and Savior, we come to an understanding that we must submit all to God, who is superior to us. This is often a fight because Satan wants to keep us separated from

God. But when we truly believe the revelation that God is Abba, our inseparable Father, we submit to Abba's leading in our lives no matter what temptations Satan brings before us. Any temptations, offenses, or fears that come our way we will overcome because our submission, respect, and reverence are fully surrendered to Abba.

Therefore if we are afraid of submission, then we are not yet worshipping God with all our heart. If we do not submit to Abba's leading, then we are not yet worshipping God. This is why our songs alone are not worship. Songs become worship to God when those singing the songs are submitted to God, even after finishing them. Worship is when we get up and go do what God is telling us to do. The strength of worship is submission, and it makes us fully inseparable from our Father. When we submit to God, He becomes our source of strength. Bible giants such as Moses, Elijah, Esther, David, and Deborah all had one thing in common: they were submitted. Submission gave these ordinary men and women the power to do extraordinary exploits for God. Likewise we must commit to worshipping God through submission. Commit to surrendering everything—your past, present, and future. Then when you hear His voice tell you which way to go or feel His rhythm leaning in a particular direction, say yes and follow. Do what He is calling you to do. This is how we become one with our Father.

Bowing and submitting to Abba may seem hard, but this is why the Holy Spirit is such a blessing to us. The Holy Spirit is the presence of God living on the inside of us as believers of God through Jesus Christ. When we pursue intimacy with God through worship, the Holy

Spirit is available and ready to help us. The Holy Spirit can help us bow because He is the spirit of truth. The Holy Spirit can help provide us with the truth of Abba's identity so our minds can submit to being completely dependent on Him. The Holy Spirit can teach us how to give God a total and complete yes in submission because He is a teacher. We do not have to walk this journey of worship alone. Abba is our inseparable Father; this means He will not leave us on our own to figure things out. God gives us the Holy Spirit, the Counselor, to help us encounter His holiness, truth, purity, love, purpose, and submission, which fill us with adoration for Abba. This is what Paul meant when He said we must walk by the Holy Spirit or else live by our own flesh, which has the power to lead us into sin, failure, abandonment, and ultimately hell (Gal. 5:16). When we believe that God is Abba, our inseparable Father, it must consume us. When we pursue being one with our Father through worship, it literally must become our hearts' cry and our minds' truth every single second of our lives. When we give ourselves to being consumed with worship, encountering Abba in the leading of the Holy Spirit, we truly receive the life-giving prayer that Jesus prayed for us. We become one with the Father, as the Father always desired to be one with us.

WE ARE WORSHIPPERS

Our intimate pursuit of Abba leads us to the revelation of our identity as worshippers. In the body of Christ we identify the men and women on our praise-and-worship teams as worshippers. However, worshipper is the identity of every single believer of Jesus Christ, whether or not he can sing. As Abba's children our identity as worshippers ensures Abba gets all the glory, which is the greatest desire of a worshipper. The focus of worshippers is not to build an earthly kingdom for themselves but to build the kingdom of God. When our goal as Abba's sons and daughters is to build the kingdom of God, the plans and purposes of Abba prevail upon the earth, and that causes others to be drawn into relationship with God through Jesus Christ.

Our identity as worshippers develops as we find ourselves in Abba. To be found in Abba is to live inseparable from the Father. Jesus talked about how to live inseparable from the Father: "I am the vine, ye are the branches: He that abideth in me, and I in him, the same bringeth forth much fruit: for without me ye can do nothing" (John 15:5). Living inseparable from Abba requires us to abide in Him and to bear fruit. To be worshippers, our commitment is to dwell in the presence of the Lord consistently. We bow and submit to God in all areas of our lives. Through our complete pursuit of Abba's identity as our inseparable Father, we fully live in our identity as worshippers.

Abide

Embracing our identity in Abba as worshippers takes abiding. Abiding is spending time in the presence of God. For some it is sitting quickly before the Lord, but for others it may be laying prostrate, physically bowing, or taking a quiet walk in nature. However you choose to spend time in the presence of God, it should be a natural result of your pursuit of Abba.

Pursuing Abba by abiding in His presence through practices such as bowing or submitting to Him causes encounters with the Holy Spirit, who ministers to our hearts and minds about our identity as worshippers. Above anything we can do for God, He wants our hearts—which are the seats of our emotions, will, and intellect—to be rooted in His identity. Our hearts need to be rooted in Abba because our hearts drive our identity, mind-set, passions, and decisions as worshippers. If we desire to be one with our Father and fully live in our identity as worshippers, we must spend time with God so He can reprogram our hearts. As we abide in Abba, our hearts become reoriented to the hearts of sons and daughters of God, which shifts our mind-sets to want to worship our Father. Time in Abba's presence strengthens what we believe in our minds about our identity in Christ as worshippers. When we abide in the Father, our mind-sets shift because we receive the wisdom of Christ on how to worship God. As we abide in Abba's presence through worship, we also receive the peace of God in our emotions that will allow us to make the decision to worship God in our deeds, such as following God's will and passions. When we abide in our identity as worshippers of the Father, the Holy Spirit can give us revelation and direction to see God's will manifest in our present circumstances and in our futures. The more our hearts and minds are strengthened, the more confidence, wisdom, and direction we gain to walk by the power of the Holy Spirit as worshippers of our Father Abba.

Abiding in Abba's presence also includes pruning. John 15:2 says that as we abide in Abba, "every branch in me that beareth not fruit he taketh away: and every branch that beareth fruit, he purgeth it, that it may bring forth more fruit." As we seek to embrace our identity and abide in Him, God prunes us so we may receive the more of Him, our Abba, the One we worship. Pruning is when He removes everything in our lives that is not helpful to our identity. Abba will prune our insecurities so they no longer hinder us from worshipping Him as His sons and daughters. Our inadequacies that tend to drive us out of God's presence will also be pruned by Abba. As we spend time with Abba, He will cut away places of fear and anxiety, which become idols that demand our worship. Abba challenges us to open our hearts and minds to Him, removing these hindrances so He can minister healing to our past brokenness. In ministering to our past brokenness, our pruning from the Father causes us to be even more fruitful in our identity as sons and daughters who worship their Father alone.

Bear fruit

When Abba has the full leading of our hearts, we can accomplish anything. As the Spirit of God guides our lives, we have the grace to become who God created us to be. Our ultimate goal becomes to see Abba's plans and purposes prevail in every single area of our lives. The Holy Spirit will help us fulfill God's plans and purposes in our marriages, homes, families, and friendships. When the Holy Spirit leads us to bear fruit, our hearts' desire is that everything we do is to the glory of God. We will desire for our words, health, diet, and even appearance to bring glory to God. We will want our children to glorify God. We will live to invite others and see others around us come into the revelation of our inseparable Father. Life becomes so much easier because we are not striving or working out of our own efforts. We bear fruit out of a place of abiding and having been pruned by the Father.

As you abide with the Father and He prunes your heart, He will call you to bear fruit by participating in His plans and purposes. God may call you to accomplish this in the area of arts and entertainment because of the gift of creativity He has given you. Or Abba may call you to bear fruit in medicine or science, or in education or business. God may also call you to bear fruit in the church.

When we arrive in these spheres of influence, we are confident and empowered, knowing in our hearts that we have the right motives. The fruit we bear is not because we are trying to impress people or because we are trying to find worldly success. When we bear fruit from our identity as worshippers, we are in line with the plans and purposes of God, and we know it ultimately gives God the glory. The issue is that many people have tried to bear fruit on their own and have ended up making a mess of things. Trying to bear fruit apart from God leads only to frustration and toiling. We become frustrated in careers, marriages, relationships, homes, and lifestyles because they were not the plans and purposes of God for our lives. When we abide in Abba, the Holy Spirit will freely give us the plans and purposes for our lives. Not only will we receive the plans and purposes, but we will also have the strength and power of the Holy Spirit with us to bear this fruit to the glory of God. Our ultimate goals as worshippers are to glorify God and never be separated from Abba.

5

OUR MERCIFUL FATHER

Seeing What Abba Sees

And God said, Let us make man in our image, after our likeness: and let them have dominion over the fish of the sea, and over the fowl of the air, and over the cattle, and over all the earth, and over every creeping thing that creepeth upon the earth. So God created man in his own image, in the image of God created he him; male and female created he them.

∞∞∞ GENESIS 1:26–27 ∞∞∞

THERE IS A war being waged against us.

It is not a war over what we hear. It is not a war over what we do. It is not even a war to stop us from dreaming about our purpose. The biggest war being waged against us is a war on our agreement. Satan knows that whatever we come into agreement with guides our vision. Our vision, our ability to see and perceive, in turn, guides what we hear, what we understand, and what we embrace about our identity and purpose. The devil has been fighting to keep us from coming into agreement with God concerning who He is and how He sees us. We are experiencing such a major esteem crisis in the world because many have not come into agreement with how God sees them. If you fall into this group, the issue is not your abilities, your skills, your personal sin, your struggles, the time you feel you have wasted, the size of your nose, your body type, or what you regret. Those are not the sources of your self-esteem issues; they are simply fruit of an issue you have with agreement. When you do not come into agreement with how God sees you, you may do weird things to try and settle, secure, and heal your identity. However, the only way to embrace Abba and ultimately embrace your own self-image is to come into agreement with God's declaration of who you are in Him.

Up until this point of the book we have been dealing a lot with how we see Abba. We discussed He is not what we have seen in past experiences with our natural fathers or authority figures in our lives. We talked about how embracing God's identity as Abba means we need to release the definitions we have used in the past to limit God. We have even examined how society sees God in universal and broad terms as well as how these conclusions and expectations have hindered our ability to see God's real identity as Father. We have even dealt with how the devil desires for us to see God as distant in an effort to keep us away from our identity as sons and daughters of Abba. However, in attempting to understand God as Abba, dealing with how we see Him is only half the battle. We have to have more information about how He sees us in order to walk in full agreement with God concerning our identity. This is perhaps one of the most difficult truths to understand because it will require us to go back to the beginning of creation and see ourselves as God always imagined us.

A DISTORTED VISION

From God's vantage point we were always a part of the plan. Genesis 1:26–27 says, "And God said, Let us make man in our image, after our likeness: and let them have dominion over the fish of the sea, and over the fowl of the air, and over the cattle, and over all the earth, and over every creeping thing that creepeth upon the earth. So God created man in his own image, in the image of God created he him; male and female created he them." At the beginning of creation God made a plan for every single human being who would ever be conceived on the earth. Abba's plan was for you and me to look just like Him. God accomplished this plan by creating humans, both male and female, in His image and in His likeness. We were a good plan; in fact, we were so good a plan in God's eyes that after He created human beings, the Bible says God looked, "And God saw every thing that he had made, and, behold, it was very good" (Gen. 1:31). From the very beginning God saw human beings as good.

Just two chapters later, in Genesis 3, which records when sin entered the earth, one of the first things that went under attack by Satan was image and likeness. The devil did not just attack what God thinks about us; he attacked what we believe about how God sees us. This attack gave us a distorted vision. We know this is true because when sin came into the planet, the first thing Adam did was run and hide from the Lord. Genesis 3:9–10 says, "And the LORD God called unto Adam, and said unto him, Where art thou? And he said, I heard thy voice in the garden, and I was afraid, because I was naked; and I hid myself." Have you ever questioned why Adam ran and hid? Maybe Adam ran because he thought God was going to be surprised at how he looked. But this could not have been the reason because God created Adam and knew how he looked. Adam said he heard God coming, so he ran and hid, but it was not so he did not have to face the repercussions of what he did. No, that was not Adam's issue. He ran because he thought he had changed in God's eyes. Adam believed that where he had been, what he had seen, what he had done, and the conversations he had had with the serpent had altered and affected how God viewed him. So Adam ran and hid because he thought that would keep God from seeing a change in him.

Adam was afraid, he was naked, and he hid. Adam's reaction tells us that our being made in God's image and likeness is not physical. Often when we think of the concept of God making us in His own image and likeness, we think of two hands, a nose, fingers, and toes. However, when God says we are made in His image and in His likeness, He is speaking about the parts of us that are immaterial in addition to the material. This is our souls, our flesh, and our spirits. When sin and sinfulness came into the world, not only was our record in heaven messed up, but our soul, flesh, and spirit collaborative became disjointed. Adam's soul was scared, his flesh was naked, and his spirit man hid. What this means is that every part of our threefold being that was supposed to be united, just as God the Father, Son, and Holy Spirit are united, took on its own agenda. Our souls started doing one thing, our flesh started doing another thing, and our spirits were desperately craving to get them both under control. The result was that we lost the ability to remember how Abba saw us before the fall. Sin completely distorted our vision and fragmented our souls, flesh, and spirits.

"I AM NOT BIASED"

Since the fall of Adam and Eve in the Garden of Eden into a life of sin we have struggled to see and believe what God really sees when He looks at us. It left room for us to think that God views each and every one of us differently based on our sin and that He measures us against others as He stands in constant judgment of us and our actions. This idea has discouraged us from turning to God for our identity. Many people have grasped instead other things trying to find their identity. As a people we have searched everywhere for our image and likeness or some resemblance of it in almost anything imaginable. Often the only thing we have settled on to fill our identity has been pain, fear, and the lust of this world. Unfortunately these things have left us with an even greater distortion of our identity. Our distorted view causes us to have biases toward others and ourselves. In our brokenness we simply project our views on Abba as if His vision is distorted and conclude that God is biased and shows partiality.

When our view of how Abba sees us is distorted, we often use our pain as a source for our identity. The pain of the past, including pain in our childhood, can seem to be an attractive fit for our identity. Wounds caused by our parents, guardians, siblings, or others can make us think, "This pain is who I am and who I am called to be forever." When pain is our identity, it becomes what we expect from life. We come to expect that everything will lead to the same brokenness or sad memories we experienced in the past. The inclination is to focus on our victimization rather than God. If we do not focus on God, the pain ends up killing our self-image. We see ourselves from the vantage point of what others have done to us and not how God sees us. When our pain is not dealt with, the wounds of the past will over time give way to regret, bitterness, and ultimately our placing blame on God.

An identity rooted in pain is selective in how it tends to view others and offenses. Pain that has not been dealt with causes us to have biases in our lives. We tend to have a bias toward people and circumstances that leave us with more pain. We fall into cycles of bad relationships and wounds. When our identity is sourced from pain, we are selective in whom we will forgive and what we will remember. When we have a bad experience or a betrayal, or something goes wrong with a person, all the good memories tend to go out the window, and only the painful experience remains. This makes the moment of pain more inflammatory because we have nothing positive with which to balance the experience. We tend to

excuse ourselves, while we sentence others to be crucified, punished, and penalized for their offenses against
us. Then we are automatically biased against anyone
who reminds us of our pain, and we treat them differently. We will even blame God for not protecting us or
for selecting the side of our accuser rather than ours as
the victim, thinking God is biased against us. However,
God is not biased against others or us. Abba is righteous,
principled, and fair. He can see in your pain—pain you
have caused and pain you have experienced at the hands
of others—and in His mercy love you just the same.

Fear is another method the devil uses to keep us
from seeing ourselves as God sees us. When we are clue-
less about how Abba sees us, we fill our identity with
fear and thoughts rooted in our fears. Remember Adam's
reaction in the garden? When sin entered in and Adam
lost knowledge of his identity in God, he grasped for
fear. Adam was afraid God would be angry and upset,
which would cause the Lord to have a different view of
him. This was completely not the case. God was upset
with Satan for tricking His creation. Adam was afraid
God would have been biased against him because of his
sin. This was not true because God is not biased. God is
consistent. Circumstances do not change God's views or
perspectives concerning us. The reality was that God still
cared for Adam and his wife, Eve. Even though there
were consequences to their actions, God's anger was
directed at the serpent rather than them. As we learn
to see God as Abba, we are going to find out that fear
is the foremost hindrance to seeing ourselves as God
sees us. I believe fear is even stronger than rejection and
abandonment in deterring us from our true identity in

God because it keeps us in cycles where we hide behind inaccurate, negative, and distorted views of ourselves. Because we are hiding, truth can miss us if we do not choose to come out of agreement with fear to agree with Abba and His vision for our lives.

When people have an incorrect view of how Abba sees them, some will grasp for the lust of the world to fill their identity. This is when we retrieve sources of validity and of value from the things around us. We see ourselves through the shattered lens of "I am what I do." Our identity is centered around our accolades, what we can accomplish, where we have gone to school, what community we live in, the number of college degrees we have, how much money we make, and how many things we have accumulated. Then we use these material gains to discriminate against others. We are biased against those who did not go to college or did not attend our college. We are biased toward those in a different income bracket than ours or those who live in a different neighborhood. If we retrieve security in our identity through our accomplishments, abilities, or capabilities, then our identity will be under siege if anything threatens these factors. In addition, when what we believe about how God sees us is under siege, everything in our world can be stolen, trifled, or taken from us. Rather than seeing ourselves through the idea of "I am what I do" and our distorted skills and accomplishments, God desires for us to see ourselves in light of "I do because I am." God wants us to see that everything He gives us—our skills and abilities—is because of who we are in Him. Our identity as sons and daughters is the priority for Abba, even before our assignments, ministries, or calls.

A MERCIFUL FATHER

The truth is no matter how we feel about ourselves at any moment or what we choose to believe about our image and likeness, Abba's thoughts toward us never change. This is because when God sees us, He sees the potential for all of us to become like His Son! Jesus makes every person valuable to God. This is why the objective of sanctification is not to make sure we are pretty; it is not about our body type or how much we weigh. Sanctification is about our spirits, bodies, and souls coming into agreement with Christ so we can see ourselves as God sees us. The objective of sanctification is for us to agree that we are Abba's sons and daughters. Sanctification's goal is for us to come into agreement with the idea that God loves us with an everlasting love. Sanctification itself is the testimony that despite our inconsistencies, unfaithfulness, sin, struggles, fears, pain, regrets, and lust for the things of this world God is merciful. He is fair and principled in how He views everyone. Every time He looks at us, He chooses to see the potential in us to become like Jesus. Through the hope of sanctification when we become believers in God through Jesus Christ, Abba sees us as sons and daughters. When God looks at us from His vantage point in heaven, it is His own image and His own likeness that shine brightly back to Him.

Abba is merciful in how He sees us because He is just. Mercy is basically God's expression of value. God only grants mercy to something He thinks is important. When God shows us mercy, it says we mean something to Him. God would never give somebody mercy if He doubted his willingness to change a circumstance, a decision, or a scenario. God will extend mercy to us because He is hopeful that when we come into the realization of who we are in Christ, we will want to live with Him as our Abba Father. Abba believed in this plan so much that He inspired Ezekiel to prophesy about it in the Old Testament:

> None eye pitied thee, to do any of these unto thee, to have compassion upon thee; but thou wast cast out in the open field, to the lothing of thy person, in the day that thou wast born. And when I passed by thee, and saw thee polluted in thine own blood, I said unto thee when thou wast in thy blood, Live; yea, I said unto thee when thou wast in thy blood, Live. I have caused thee to multiply as the bud of the field, and thou hast increased and waxen great, and thou art come to excellent ornaments: thy breasts are fashioned, and thine hair is grown, whereas thou wast naked and bare. Now when I passed by thee, and looked upon thee, behold, thy time was the time of love; and I spread my skirt over thee, and covered thy nakedness: yea, I sware unto thee, and entered into a covenant with thee, saith the Lord GOD, and thou becamest mine.
>
> —EZEKIEL 16:5–8

Our own sins and the sins of our forefathers left us broken, naked, and afraid. Ezekiel says no one took pity on our bloody condition and the world left us to die. When this happened, Abba did not call for nurses; He did not leave us in our condition for others to come and administer CPR. Abba Himself came in the image of Christ to declare that we will live! This is because Abba is just and honorable. He could not stand by as He saw us, His creation, dying. Abba was not afraid of the dirt on us, the mess we had made, or the blood from Satan's attempts to kill us with pain and trauma. Abba looked at the condition hell had gotten us into and declared He would get the hell out of us! In His mercy He did not focus on the addictions, struggles, or wounds that got us into our condition. He never even second-guessed His actions or questioned what He would do on our behalf. When Abba saw us, He declared we would live! Abba saw potential in us to become like His Son. Out of the mercy of His heart and because He is totally fair, He did not even spare His own Son to help us from the mess of sin upon the earth. Abba released the miracle of Jesus Christ to save us from a bloody mess. This is what He did for us in Christ because He is a just Father full of mercy.

Ezekiel then goes on to explain that the first time God saw us in Christ, it was to save us. It was a gaze of compassion and mercy that brought us eternal life. The issue is that many of us stop our relationship with God at this point. We pitch a tent at salvation and stay there for the rest of our lives. But the prophet Ezekiel said Abba's plan was never for us to stop at salvation. Abba wants us to keep going past salvation to pursue righteousness. God's plan is for you to stick close by Him and for Him to become inseparable from you! Ezekiel 16:7 says Abba's plan is to multiply you, cause you to increase, prune the mistakes of the past, and heal your wounds in a place of naked vulnerability with Him. Abba's plan is to love you forever. God's desire is to cover your shame and pledge His undying love to you. The definitive goal of the plan Ezekiel notes is for Father God to enter "into a covenant with thee, saith the Lord GOD, and thou becamest mine" (Ezek. 16:8). Abba's ultimate vision is for us to agree that He will be our Father and we will be His children!

The majority of people who hear this will say, "Wow! Amazing! I can agree with this plan. Where do I sign up?" However, some may be skeptical and want to know God's motive for being a merciful Father. What did God see in them the first time He passed by and declared, "Live" (Ezek. 16:6)? In the Book of Galatians Paul gave the answer. Galatians 1:15–16 says, "But when it pleased God, who separated me from my mother's womb, and called me by his grace, to reveal his Son in me, that I might preach him among the heathen; immediately I conferred not with flesh and blood." These verses explain that God was pleased to save you, to become your Abba, to declare that you shall live and not die, because He is merciful, gracious, and good. As evidenced by the sheer mercy of God, Abba valued you as someone important, as someone worth saving. It pleased Abba to live the very identity of who He is as a merciful Father to save you. It pleased Him to show mercy and to save you because He sees you as valuable. Abba sees you as worth it! So when God saw you, He was willing to save you and come into agreement with you because underneath the filth of sin you resembled His Son. Since you resembled His son, God extended you the mercy of Christ.

Abba was not motivated to save you because of what you would do for the kingdom of God. Abba was not motivated to save you so He would win against His enemy. He was not motivated to save you because He could gain praise, worship, or honor from you. The pure love of Abba reveals that God's overflowing mercy was Abba's only motivating factor. Think about it; for something to be revealed, it has to come from something else. Abba's love reveals that He is a merciful Father. In the same way, Paul tells us it was the mercy of God that reveals to us our identity. Abba knew our identity all along because it reflected Christ. God saw Christ's reflection within us because Christ reveals the perfect expression of Abba's image and likeness. Thus, God's mercy revealed what He always saw in you. His mercy revealed that Abba always saw in you the reflection of Himself.

For that reason when Abba sees you, He thinks, "That boy looks familiar," or "That girl looks familiar." When Abba looks upon us with His gaze of compassion, it is a result of nothing other than His mercy. Not even your highest potential could have persuaded God to save you. As a matter of fact, Isaiah 64:6 says that "all our righteousnesses are as filthy rags" to God. There is nothing we can do in our own strength to win the Father's love or change His view concerning us! There is no career we can choose or status we can achieve that could ever change God's opinion about us. There is no mistake or sin too big to cause God to change His mind about us. Paul said God "was pleased to reveal his Son to me" (Gal. 1:15–16, ESV). God is always pleased to reveal the Son because He helps us see what Abba sees when He looks at us. It pleases God to reveal Christ because when we look at Christ, we should see our reflection. We should be able to look at Christ and know that when Abba looks at us, He does not see the resemblances of

His foe. No! Abba sees the remembrances of His Son. The good news is that Abba is a sucker for His Son, and He loves us just as much!

Thanks be to God that Jesus Christ is in us through the Holy Spirit (Gal. 2:20). Sometimes He is trying to live in us past our tendencies for sin, drug use, issues with overspending, generational issues, or insecurities. However, through the Holy Spirit, Christ lives within us, and because of His resemblance in us God acts and moves on our behalf. You may not be able to see it now, but God desires for us to know that we are a reflection of Him. So Abba will continue to extend His mercy to us because, as any good father knows, when individuals are young, it is hard for them to see that they resemble their parent, no matter how much you tell them. Though the children cannot see the resemblance, the father does not love the children any less. No, the father continues to nurture the children and encourages them to live, knowing that over time the children will develop and mature and their features will grow. Then one day the children will finally look in the mirror and agree, "I do look like my father. I do resemble him, just as others say." This is the hope our merciful Father has for us. Abba continues to hope, believe, and trust that one day we too will agree that we are Abba's children and are called to be His reflection on Earth.

PURSUE RIGHTEOUSNESS

The mercy of God is truly unmatched! When we, through His mercy, walk in agreement with God, fully secure in Abba's identity and with the knowledge that

He sees Christ in us, we are unstoppable! This is why the devil fights to keep us separated from God and out of agreement with Him so much. He knows the last time someone who looked like us walked in full agreement with God and lived on the earth, He was able to turn Satan's kingdom upside down! Jesus was always in total agreement with the Father, so God gave Him the power to destroy the works of sin. Hence Satan fights our agreement and promotes our having a distorted view of God because He does not want us to respond to the power of Abba's vision for us to become sons and daughters. He does not want us to have the power to see what Abba sees. When we agree with how Abba sees us, God is able to take His position as Lord over every area in our lives. This makes us more powerful than any obstacle or sin that would seek to hinder us. We respond to how Abba sees us and His mercy by pursuing righteousness, which, as mentioned, was His original plan for us. We pursue righteousness by renewing our minds with the truth about what God sees when He sees us.

To pursue righteousness means to seek after being in right standing with Abba. Our righteousness, or our lack thereof, governs the way we view things and the constitutions by which we live. When we are in right standing with Abba, our ultimate aim is to have the same views as the Father at all times concerning all things, including how we view ourselves. When we actively pursue righteousness in our lives, it affects our values, beliefs, and habits. We go about pursuing righteousness by renewing our minds. Renewing our minds is so important because we need to exchange our old ways of seeing ourselves for how God sees us. We renew our minds through the reading, rehearsing, and researching of the Word of God. We can be assured that our pursuit to renew our minds will give us the values of God concerning us, and it will also help us to hold the same beliefs and habits about ourselves that Abba has.

Reading the Word of God will give you an even greater understanding of Abba and His desire for you to be like His son. Philippians 2:5 reads, "Let this mind be in you, which was also in Christ Jesus." Abba's hope is that you would have the same mind that is in Christ and that you would think of yourself as Christ does and that you would see yourself as a son or daughter as Christ sees Himself as a son. This type of thinking requires that you fill yourself with the Word of God. The Word of God helps you gain the information needed for the Holy Spirit to begin the change process in your mind and mind-set. The more Scripture you read, the better. By the mercy of God you receive the correct vision for both Abba and yourself when you read the Word of God.

Growing in how God sees you will take rehearsing God's Word over your life. You need to renew your thinking from a distorted vision of yourself to a whole vision of yourself in Abba. You must spend time believing promises God says about you and how He sees you. When you rehearse Scripture over your life, you give them permission to exist in your life. In consistent communication with the Father you can ask Him for specific scriptures that He wants you to focus on concerning areas in your life where you are struggling to receive His view. You can engage and rely on the Holy Spirit to help lead you to the truth of God's love for you as His son or daughter. Rehearse His mercy for you. Rehearse

His compassion for you. Rehearse His dislikes. Let it become life-giving to you. Rehearse closeness to Him. Researching is also another way to pursue the righteousness of God through the renewing of our minds. You can spend time in Scripture researching different topics concerning how God views you and the immensity of His love for you as a son or daughter.

WE ARE LIKE-MINDED

Our pursuit of righteousness leads us into our own identity. We are called to be sons and daughters of Abba who are like-minded, or of one mind, with our Father. To be like-minded is to walk in total agreement with Abba through the lordship of Christ. When we fully live in our identity to be like-minded, we can see what Abba sees at all times regarding ourselves, our circumstances, and others because we are fully submitted to Christ, the One after whom Abba desires we model our lives. As a merciful Father, Abba desires to teach us His view of us, which has the power to heal our identity. How God sees us is often hard to grasp because it requires us to come out of agreement with our old, distorted views of ourselves and come into agreement, or become like-minded, with Abba's view. We must prioritize His vision for our lives, our careers, our families, and our decisions over other things in life that compete for our vision or that require our attention. We prioritize by making Christ the Lord over our lives. The truth of how God sees us can also be hard because often in our churches we are taught that Abba only looks at our sin. There are whole churches that build their foundations on a heavy focus of sin and the consequences of hell. Even though sin and hell are very real, focusing solely on those two aspects of the Bible causes people to have identity issues because they are so busy dealing with the guilt, shame, and condemnation from sin that they cannot walk in agreement with the lordship of Christ. Walking in that agreement allows us to access Abba's mercy, which sees us as sons and daughters. Above and beyond our sin Abba sees in us the potential to become like His Son, Jesus. A lot of people have asked me if Father God is blind to our sin because He sees His Son in us. But it is not that Abba is ignorant of our sins or blind to our wrongdoings. He just chooses to see the best in us. Abba chooses to see that part of you He is invested in, the part of you that looks like Jesus.

In Christ's lordship we will always live as like-minded sons and daughters of Abba who are healed and whole in our identity. In 2 Peter 1:3 the Bible says, "According as his divine power hath given unto us all things that pertain unto life and godliness, through the knowledge of him that hath called us to glory and virtue." As believers of Jesus Christ, everything God gives us is assigned to help us fully live in our identity as like-minded people or to live as individuals who can see without a shadow of a doubt that Abba made us to be like Christ. God gives us gifts, powers, and abilities, and anoints us for godliness so we can see ourselves like Christ and become like-minded in our vision to live as He did, in total agreement with Abba. If heaven has a way to send things to us on the earth, it is through our gifts, powers, abilities, and anointing. They are the means by which God provides us with the resources to become like-minded or to walk in agreement with Abba's vision of Christ's likeness within us. Consequently if we fail to become like-minded with Abba and we fail to see ourselves as Abba sees us, then we have restricted our access to the resources God assigned for our lives.

The blessing for us today is that we have the full measure of the Holy Spirit to help us live completely under Christ's lordship and thus become like-minded in our identity as Abba's sons and daughters. As we pursue righteousness, by God's mercy we will gain the victory against every enemy seeking to blind us to Abba's identity and His vision for us. Remember, Satan is against our becoming like-minded with God's idea of how He made us and how He sees us. However, we partner with the Holy Spirit to keep Christ as Lord of every area of our lives. To be like-minded in our identity is to live as Jesus said He did: "Then answered Jesus and said unto them, Verily, verily, I say unto you, The Son can do nothing of himself, but what he seeth the Father do: for what things soever he doeth, these also doeth the Son likewise" (John 5:19). When we fully live in our identity as like-minded sons and daughters of Abba, we will have similar or identical opinions, dispositions, and even vision to Abba. When we come into agreement with Abba's vision we will have the same urgency in our hearts as Christ to do as Abba does and see as Abba sees. We will be like-minded in Christ as we pursue righteousness to fully believe how Abba sees us and to agree with Abba's vision for our lives. Through the power of the Holy Spirit Abba will grant us the confidence to live, grow, and multiply in His love and vision for us as sons and daughters. When we commit to surrendering to what Abba sees in us, the Father will even bring individuals into our lives to unlock the dormant resources within us. Abba will send us individuals who can help us recognize, develop, and unlock who God always made us to be in Christ.

I believe the revelation of how Abba sees us is so crucial to the success of our lives that it should be the first thing new Christians learn. Those who have surrendered to Christ's lordship in their lives should immediately begin to learn how Abba sees them and His vision for their lives as sons and daughters. I believe that as new converts learn their identity to become like-minded, their relationship with Abba will blossom richly out of a love for Him and a pursuit of righteousness that leads to their doing as God does and seeing as God sees. This is so important because Abba's identity and how we believe Abba sees us affect everything in our lives. They affect how we pray, worship, read the Bible, care for the poor, serve, love our neighbors, live, run our households, make decisions, and even steward money. We should ask new members in our church questions such as, "How do you see Abba? What do you believe Abba sees about you?" Then, once they properly understand how Abba views them, we can begin to equip them in principles, including prayer, fasting, and witnessing. With the right view of Abba and an identity that is like-minded to Christ, fasting is easy. Prayer? Easy. Sharing your faith with others? Easy. These spiritual disciplines become very easy for those who are like-minded in their identity of how Abba views them and views Himself. No one has to coerce such individuals to be like Christ in the earth. They willfully embrace the responsibility of being Abba's sons and daughters who reveal Christ to the world.

The declaration of those who are like-minded with God or who receive the revelation of how Abba sees them in Christ is found in Galatians 2:20. Paul wrote, "I am crucified with Christ: nevertheless I live; yet not I, but Christ liveth in me: and the life which I now live in the flesh I live by the faith of the Son of God, who loved me, and gave himself for me." When we see ourselves as Abba sees us, every issue in our identity is healed! When our identity is healed, we can reach our highest potential and our highest destiny, which is to be a reflection of Jesus upon the earth. As we focus on our identity to be like-minded with Christ, the enemies of our souls—sin, depression, and heaviness—are destroyed and our identity and likeness are restored; we become the vision Abba always saw in us as His sons and daughters. Let us never forget that Abba sees us in the light of Christ. Let us remember that God believes in us and is committed to protecting Christ's image in us and protecting our identity in Him.

6

OUR PROTECTIVE FATHER

We Are Secured

The name of the LORD is a strong tower: the
righteous runneth into it, and is safe.

∞∞∞ PROVERBS 18:10 ∞∞∞

ABBA IS COMMITTED to protecting the image of
Christ in us and our identity in Him. God is
committed to protecting our identity from the ongoing
internal spiritual attacks of Satan against us. These spiritual attacks seek to steal our agreement with our identity
and our confidence in God. One area of our confidence
that comes under great attack is our belief in Abba's protection of us. We face internal attacks that cause us to ask
questions such as, "Will Abba protect me when I need
protection?" Satan never misses the chance to present
us with this question to drive distrust against God in

our hearts. Satan likes to push us to ask this question particularly in times of uncertainty, in inordinate darkness, and when we are on the brink of taking big risks for God. Our answer to this question reveals what we believe about Jesus and what we believe He accomplished on the cross. Our response also reveals the current state of our heart and whether or not it is fearful and wavering or secured in godly confidence.

What is interesting about the internal struggles we face is that we already have the victory over them in Christ. Second Corinthians 2:14 reminds us, "Now thanks be unto God, which always causeth us to triumph in Christ, and maketh manifest the savour of his knowledge by us in every place." In Jesus's death and resurrection He gained victory for us. This victory is not only sometimes or over some things. Scripture says Jesus's victory is always available for every battle we ever face. Jesus became our champion over sin and death as well as every other struggle we face, both natural and spiritual. Jesus guarantees Abba's protection for us so we can have this victory in every battle. If through Christ we already have the victory, then why do we have to engage in these internal struggles? Well, the internal fight is over our belief in what Christ did for us on the cross. If you do not believe that you have the victory through Christ, then you live as if you are defeated. And this is Satan's goal, that you would live defeated, unsure of God's desire to protect you, and ignorant of your identity as victorious in Christ.

THE DAILY ATTACK

Our hearts and minds are inundated every moment of the day with information. We receive both external and internal inputs that we must process for every decision we make. External inputs include things such as the news or advice from a spouse or friend. Our culture, history, and education also provide input in our decision-making processes. Part of the internal inputs we receive come by way of questions. Some of these questions arise in our minds from thoughts, attitudes, and beliefs we have in our hearts. Our vulnerabilities and insecurities are also internal inputs that raise questions when we have decisions to make. The plan of Satan has been to use our internal thoughts, especially our vulnerabilities and insecurities, to drive questions that lead us to doubt God because when we doubt God, any number of Satan's goals become possible. We can end up in disobedience, rebellion, or any other thing that falls out of the will of God. Satan works every single day to try and get us to focus on our vulnerabilities and insecurities. His hope is that by getting us to doubt God by focusing on ourselves, we will forfeit the victory we have in Jesus and live a defeated life.

Satan's attack on humanity began in the Garden of Eden. All the serpent did was ask a question, but that question was able to highlight the doubt in Adam's and Eve's hearts that eventually led them to fall into sin. Genesis 3:1 reads, "Now the serpent was more cunning than any beast of the field which the LORD God had made. And he said to the woman, 'Has God indeed said, "You shall not eat of every tree of the garden"?'" (NKJV).

The serpent began by posing a question concerning Abba. At first it may have seemed to be an innocent question, but its motive was to lead to doubt in the hearts of Adam and Eve concerning God. In modern-day terms the serpent's question sounds like this: "Was God really protecting you when He said you could eat from every tree in the garden?" The serpent was questioning Abba's identity and motives, and He challenged Abba's words by asking if Abba really said that people should not eat of all the trees in the garden. The serpent was, in effect, attempting to question whether or not Adam and Eve were going to follow God and not eat from the tree God told them not to eat from. In addition, "Then the serpent said to the woman, 'You will not surely die. For God knows that in the day you eat of it your eyes will be opened, and you will be like God, knowing good and evil'" (Gen. 3:4–5, NKJV). Not only did the serpent raise doubts about God, but he also presented Adam and Eve with an alternative position against what God instructed them.

Ultimately Adam and Eve left the serpent's question unanswered. They did not counter the lies of Satan with the truth that God was indeed protecting them with His instructions. I believe that Genesis 3 reveals a great deal about Adam's and Eve's hearts. The devil found something in their hearts that was prone to agree with his lies. The fact that Adam and Eve were willing to entertain the serpent's conversation about God leaves us to wonder if Adam and Eve already had these questions in their hearts, whether it was a fleeting thought or a deep-seated concern that God was withholding something good from them. Perhaps they were questioning God's motives as well. Satan simply gave voice to the insecurities and vulnerabilities that were already present in their hearts. When these questions, insecurities, and vulnerabilities were left unaddressed by Abba's truth, Satan took the opportunity to present an alternative position to God's truth. The serpent's question and lies led to the disintegration of Adam's and Eve's faith in God. They traded God's wisdom for their own wisdom, which introduced sin and humanism to the human race.

This same plan of attack continues to be waged against us daily. This is Satan's whole playbook: to seed a thought or question in our minds that exploits some undecided part of our souls that does not fully trust in Abba's protection. After that Satan traps us in a cycle of uncontrolled emotions and poor decisions inspired by doubt that comes from our insecurities and vulnerabilities. Hence our goal in life is to become fully confident in Abba, in His identity as our protector, and in our identity as victors because of Christ's finished work on the cross. Growing in our faith and trusting in Abba's protection would keep us from taking wrong turns in life, becoming distracted by trivial matters, and falling into sin.

"I AM NOT YOUR VULNERABILITIES AND INSECURITIES"

Jesus knew all too well the devastation that Satan's plan was causing in the earth. He saw the sick, the hungry, and the greedy. He saw the empty rituals of religion and knew humanity needed help. Even though Jesus was going to leave as a conqueror over Satan's attack against Him, He recognized we would need protection to overcome Satan's daily attacks against us to doubt God. Jesus prayed, "I will remain in the world no longer, but they are still in the world, and I am coming to you. Holy Father, protect them by the power of your name, the name you gave me, so that they may be one as we are one" (John 17:11, NIV). Jesus was concerned about the vulnerabilities and insecurities that threaten the hearts of Abba's sons and daughters. Jesus is found here making intercession for us because he knows Satan can use our vulnerabilities and insecurities to cause us to question Abba's identity and take an alternative position that perverts our faith and positions it against God.

Whether we realize it or not, our vulnerabilities and insecurities play a powerful role in our actions and relationship with God. Our places of vulnerability and insecurity can stem from different sources. They can come as a factor of our experiences. For example, if someone takes an exam, and everyone in his class passed except him, he will experience a vulnerable moment through which insecurities can enter his life, such as those concerning his grades or his level of intelligence. Insecurities have a way of compounding. For example, this man's insecurities about his grades and intelligence can lead to a fear of test taking, withdrawal from classmates because he does not believe he is smart enough to be around them, or even depression. Ultimately these vulnerabilities and insecurities that arise causes the student to question if God is protecting him or if God cares about him and his grades. At every point of the scenario you can be sure that Satan is bringing up questions leading the student even deeper into defeat. Satan will use these moments in our lives to bring up questions concerning

God's identity and to drive doubt in our hearts against God and His ability to protect us.

Past traumas are another source of our vulnerabilities and insecurities. When we face traumas during vulnerable moments in our lives, insecurities rooted in fear are created. These fears affect both our actions and our views of God. For example, a man may internalize fear after watching his father leave his family when he was a child. If this insecurity is not addressed as he grows up, it becomes the basis for him to question if he can be committed in a relationship or if he is good enough to marry, or to fear that whomever he marries will leave him. These insecurities can lead him to view God in light of this trauma. Often victims of trauma will question where God was in the midst of their traumatic experience. We ourselves may question why God did not do anything to help or to stop a particular trauma from occurring to us or others. This *why* question is human nature, and we all ask it. It is easy in these moments to take the insecurities we are facing and place them on God and blame Him for the experiences we have encountered that have brought fear and pain into our lives. It is easy to reason that our vulnerabilities and insecurities are bigger than God and that He is no better than our victimizers or those who make a decision to bring fear and pain into the lives of others.

However, God is not our vulnerabilities and insecurities. Our vulnerabilities and insecurities are a form of fear, and God is perfect love. There is no fear within Him because His perfect love casts out fear (1 John 4:18). Abba cannot be our vulnerabilities and insecurities; He longs to be our protector. The interesting thing about our vulnerabilities and insecurities is they signal some kind of danger to us; they instruct us to take some protective action. The issue is that we seek protection in things that are unhealthy for us, such as worry, fear, anxiety, food, or worse instead of seeking protection in God. When we seek protection in things outside of God, we get stuck in cycles of depression, fear, anxiety, and heartbreak that lead to more vulnerabilities and insecurities. God is the only One who can break us out of this cycle because He is a protector. Abba's identity is to be a protector. God desires to protect us, has been protecting us, and will always protect us if we allow Him to. Abba's protection may not always be what we thought He should have done. Yet His protection has a promise. His protection is what keeps us from being totally consumed by circumstances, traumas, and Satan's plan to kill, steal, and destroy our lives. (See Lamentations 3:22.) Abba's protection is that He is exceedingly greater than any trauma we have faced, so much so that He can take our trauma, vulnerabilities, insecurities, and questions asking why and turn them into good. Abba's promise of protection in Romans 8:28 is that "we know that all things work together for good to them that love God, to them who are the called according to his purpose." Because of Christ's finished work on the cross we do not have to fear anymore. We can turn to God to be our protector because He can turn our *why me?* questions into *now what?* questions that can pave the way to a new and good purpose and perspective beyond our trauma, vulnerabilities, and insecurities. As believers of Jesus Christ we can all be secure that through the blood of Jesus we have an extra layer of proof that Abba's protection for us will not fail. No matter if we are feeling vulnerable or insecure, God is prepared to protect us. Isaiah 55:8–9 reminds us: "For my thoughts are not your thoughts, neither are your ways my ways, saith the LORD. For as the heavens are higher than the earth, so are my ways higher than your ways, and my thoughts than your thoughts." Abba's protection of us may not look the way we expect, but He always has a plan for good. If, by embracing His identity as protector and coming out of agreement with the idea that He is like our vulnerabilities and insecurities, we allow Him the opportunity to protect us, we will see a manifestation of His good plan for our lives.

A PROTECTIVE FATHER

In life there are battles that need to be fought for us, for our destiny, because we cannot do it on our own; the Lord has promised time and again that He will fight them for us. In Exodus 14:14 Moses reminded the people, "The LORD shall fight for you, and ye shall hold your peace." Abba fights for us because that is what a father does; He is a protector. Throughout the Bible God consistently demonstrates this aspect of His nature. Many people unintentionally place more weight on God as a provider than God as a protector. However, even God's expression of Himself as a provider is because He wants to protect us from the bondage of poverty, greed, and the various other symptoms of lack. Keep in mind that Abba is not Santa Claus, and He certainly is not a genie in a bottle. Just because it is on our wish list does not mean God will give it to us. Abba's first responsibility to us is to protect us, even if that means not honoring one of our desires if it could bring us harm. Abba is a protector who provides us, His children, with exactly what we need in accordance with what will keep us safe.

In the traditional family model the father is the primary provider, but he is also protector. That is, fathers protect their families from physical harm. God, on the other hand, has both the interest and capacity to protect us in every part of our existence. Abba's protection extends to our minds, hearts, souls, identity, purpose, and futures. Sometimes Abba is willing to go through uncommon means to protect us. Throughout Scripture we see Abba's identity as a protector in full display. The Old Testament refers to Abba as a "strong tower," a "fortress," and a "battle axe" (Prov. 18:10; Ps. 18:2; Jer. 51:20). These are all warfare terms to assure us that we can run to Abba at all times and in any circumstance in our lives, and God will go to war and fight on our behalf to protect us. Second Chronicles 20:20–23 details how Abba sent a confusing spirit upon Israel's enemies to safeguard them. The spirit of confusion made the enemies of Israel turn on one another and away from Israel. Even though God is not the author of confusion, which means He does not write it into His story, He still gets use of it. There is nothing that God cannot use to protect His people. He even uses His adversary, as He did in the Book of Job, to ultimately work good in our lives. When Satan came against Job and his family, the Lord was able to use Satan's plot against Job to bless him. Because of God's protection Satan could not kill Job. God blessed Job with double the blessings he had before Satan's attack on his life, and he also dealt with pride and fear in Job's heart, which had created the open door for Satan to wreak havoc in his life. Abba was able to use his adversary's plan in order to bless Job and to bring healing to his heart.

It is a challenge for many, especially those who have dealt with trauma, to believe that Abba is invested in their protection. The pain of traumatic experiences brings fears, vulnerabilities, and insecurities that make it hard for people to trust that anyone can protect them. Overcoming trauma and its aftereffects can seem impossible if we are trying to resolve them on our own. Only God can and will help us overcome the traumatic experiences of the past. Psalm 25:3, Isaiah 54:4, and Romans 10:13 are all scriptures that encourage us to trust in the Lord. When we place our trust in the Abba, He can help protect us. No matter what traumas are in our past, Abba will protect us from the outcomes and stigmas. We will never be embarrassed trusting in God, nor will we ever be put to shame. When we feel as if it is impossible to overcome Satan's plan to keep us in cycles of trauma and hopelessness, Abba will protect. There is nothing that would come against us that Abba cannot protect His children from.

This is the beautiful thing about Abba: He has innumerable ways He can protect us. The powerful thing is that He can use anything to do it. The New Testament records that Jesus said Abba protects by His name (John 17:11–12). The very first thing any father gives his child is a name, and in general we do not take our mother's last name. The greatest gift Abba gave Jesus was His name. God did not just give Jesus any name either. According to Philippians 2:9, God gave Jesus a name "that is above every name." So when Jesus was praying for our protection, He asked God to provide protection for us in the power of His name. Jesus knew His name was powerful, yet He desired so much for our protection that He asked God to protect not just in His own name (Christ), but also in Abba's name (John 17:11–12). Our protection was *that important* to Jesus. Since there is no name higher than the name of God, Jesus was revealing to us the level of commitment God has to protect us, His children. Abba's pledge and commitment to us is that with Him we are always protected. God is so committed to protecting us that He literally put His name and His reputation on the line.

PURSUE SAFETY IN ABBA

Think about how much stability we would have in life, how carefree our lives would be, if we believed God is our protector! We would not be shaken by elections, financial crises, or anything else this life can bring. Imagine what it would look like if we really made it a commitment to find ourselves in the safety of Abba, our strong tower, or if we committed to truly living in the identity of Abba's protected children. How do we accomplish this? How do we relate to Abba as protector? We relate to our protective Father by pursuing safety in Abba. We pursue safety in Abba by becoming aware of His desire to protect us and then committing to presenting Him with our every single decision and movement. Then we wait upon Him to provide us with direction before we move.

Become aware

It is our awareness of God's protection over us that allows us to cooperate with Abba. We must be aware of God's desire to protect us and then make it something we pursue every single day of our lives. When we are unaware of Abba's protection at work in our lives, we use our faith and our strength to fight against God. Imagine there is a physical altercation between two people, and a third party intervenes to break it up. Should the two parties choose to continue fighting, the third party will eventually lose interest, withdraw, and let the two continue to fight it out. Imagine that the physical altercation is between you and whoever or whatever is trying to bring fear, insecurities, vulnerabilities, or trauma your way. The third party who intervenes is God, who is seeking to protect you. When we live unaware that Abba desires to protect us, we choose to continue fighting even though He is present and willing to intervene on our behalf. At some point God withdraws and waits for us to allow Him to fight on our behalf. That is why we must become aware of His desire to protect us, so we can become willing to cooperate with Him.

I am a huge wrestling fan. When there is a two-on-two match, only one wrestling partner fights at a time. As soon as the one partner looks as if he is about to lose the match, he reaches out, tags his partner in the ring, and exits to the side. It is the same thing with God. He desires to protect us, even if it's from ourselves. He wants us to tag Him into every fight we face. This is Abba's grace, and it is a protective mechanism. Our job is to respond by getting out of the way and letting Abba protect us. This is why Moses said, "The LORD shall fight for you, and ye shall hold your peace" (Exod. 14:14). To hold our peace is to acknowledge that Abba is our protector and to get out of the way and let Him fight on our behalf.

When we get out of the way and let Abba fight our battles, we will always come out victorious. The prophets in Israel frequently encouraged the nation to get out of God's way for Him to fight their battles. During times of war the prophets would say, "Stand still, and see the salvation of the LORD." (See Exodus 14:13; 2 Chronicles 20:17.) The word for salvation in the Hebrew is *yeshuwah*, meaning "deliverance, welfare, prosperity, and victory."[1] The prophets were not telling the people to stand in the midst of the battle and give up. No! They were encouraging the people to become aware of God's protection and to watch Him give them the victory over their enemies. Standing still did not necessarily mean they stood around and played hopscotch. At times they would engage with their enemy, and at other times they would simply lift up their voices and praise God. Standing still means to rest in the promise and protection of Abba, to still the anxious mind and the fearful and worried heart. The Hebrew *yeshuwah*, or Yeshua, is translated to the Greek as "Jesus." Our job is not to try and figure out how God will handle our situations. Our task is to focus on Jesus and move in the direction of Abba's deliverance, welfare, prosperity, and victory over our enemies.

Present our decisions and movements

Once we acknowledge the protection Abba offers, we must present all our decisions and movements to Him.

We present our decisions and movements to Him in prayer. We do so by asking Abba for clarity on all of our decisions and about all of things we desire to do. For example, if we have an upcoming decision to make about work, we can pray and ask God for clarity on what move we should make on our job. Or if we are experiencing a place of vulnerability or insecurity that is causing us to ask, "Why did this happen?" or "Why didn't You stop this, God?" we can go to Abba for clarity, as we discussed earlier, and ask questions such as, "What can I learn from this?" "What part of this experience is for my protection?" and "What other opportunities are You providing for me, Abba?" When we present all our decisions and movements to Abba, it provides protection for us because it takes the guesswork out of our lives. We can gain the Father's wisdom and save ourselves from the harm, trial and error, and unnecessary heartbreak that come from our trying to figure out life on our own. In presenting our decisions and movements to Abba, we can gain the peace and assurance of protection that we need through the clarity He provides us in a place of prayer. Think about how many people live their lives defensively and as orphans or individuals who have to fight alone in life because they have not presented their decisions and movements to Abba to receive His peace and clarity. They are missing out on the amazing blessings we receive when we relate to God as our Father and protector. Orphans miss out on the fact that Abba is a buckler, a rock, and a fortress because they are busy trying to fight every battle, every fear, anxiety, worry, depression, decision, or circumstance on their own. Yet Abba does not want us to fight on our own. This is why

He uses all these military and warfare terms to describe Himself. He wants us to present our decisions and movements to Him and trust that He can provide us with the clarity that can shield us or act as a fortress for us against any unnecessary consequences.

No human being would want to be known as an inanimate object. I would never tell you to call me a vase or call me a cabinet unless it painted a picture to help you understand my motives. In the same way studying the nicknames of God can help orphans understand who Abba desires them to be and encourage them to present their decisions and movements to Him in a place of prayer. Studying in this way will help us all remember to present our decisions and movements to Abba's protection for our lives as well. Statements such as "Abba is your shield" are revelations of His motives toward His people. It is Abba's desire to shield us from whatever our lives may bring. You will learn that our Father says, "I am your buckler. I am your very present help" (Ps. 18:30; 46:1). A buckler is a protective shield worn on the left arm of a person to protect his body.[2] Therefore Abba wants us, His children, to know that He is no further than an arm's length away, present and available to help us in whatever situation we are facing. Against all the odds Abba will protect His people. God can and will use any and all methods and means to protect those who pursue His protection. The more we pursue God's safety and present our decisions and movements to Him, the more of His protection Abba reveals to us. Now that we are aware of Abba's desire to protect, we must present all our decisions and movements to Him and watch as He provides direction for us.

Wait on Abba's direction

We also pursue safety in Abba by waiting. Waiting is never easy. Sometimes when we present our decisions and movements to Abba in prayer, we may not hear anything from the Lord. In those moments the temptation is to move with our own wisdom and go with our own passion. We are tempted to do this because it seems as if Abba is not available, does not care, or is unwilling to help us. But when we step out on our own, we risk experiencing negative consequences because we did not want to wait on God. Abba's direction is a sign of His desire to protect us because He does not want us having to figure out life on our own. When Abba calls on us to wait on His direction, we have to trust that there is safety in the waiting because Abba will always provide direction for us when we ask Him, as that is in line with His identity as a protector. When we receive Abba as a protector, this grants Him permission to do and be whatever He needs to do and be in our lives to protect us. Sometimes the direction Abba leads us to is to wait on Him, which can seem unconventional, but it can always be trusted.

The danger is when we learn that Abba is a protector but do not believe it and do not wait and trust in Him to provide direction. To not wait and trust God makes us a welcome mat for our adversaries. The things we are afraid of will begin to happen because we have mustered our faith in the wrong direction. Remember, fear is perverse faith. Faith pointed in the wrong direction is fear; it is contrary faith. Fear will cause stuff to manifest in our lives because we are still using faith, and faith makes things manifest. If God has given everybody a "measure of faith" (Rom. 12:3), then the ability to have faith is not what makes anybody a believer. That is why Jesus told us where to put our faith: "And Jesus answering saith unto them, Have faith in God" (Mark 11:22). When we sit, we have faith that the chair will hold us. If you were to fall out of a chair, it would be a shock to you because nobody forecasted or calculated that the chair would not do what it was designed to do. And so it is with our pursuit of safety in Abba through waiting—we can trust that God hears us when we pray and ask for clarity and direction and that He will protect us because that is what He does as a Father. Jesus said, "Ask, and it shall be given you; seek, and ye shall find; knock, and it shall be opened unto you: For every one that asketh receiveth; and he that seeketh findeth; and to him that knocketh it shall be opened" (Matt. 7:7–8). We can take our faith and place it in Abba and wait for Him because Jesus said that everyone who asks God will receive. So when the answers do not come as fast as we think they should, we can still have faith that waiting is the safest place for us to be because Abba loves us, sees us, and wants to protect us.

We find safety from the battles of life only when we receive God as Abba, our protector, and wait upon Him to provide clarity and direction to the questions we present Him with in a place of prayer. Waiting is not a passive pursuit; it is an active pursuit of Abba, and it requires that we be intentional in seeking God's presence and God's Word so we can listen to the leading of the Holy Spirit. The more time we spend in Abba's presence, the more we learn His voice, just as Jesus said: "My sheep hear my voice, and I know them, and they follow me" (John 10:27). This is why waiting is an active pursuit—we must continue the practice of learning and listening to Abba's voice. This way when we wait on God, we will know when Abba provides His direction because we will have the peace of knowing His voice through His Word and the leading of the Holy Spirit. Waiting is not being so paralyzed by fear that we become like orphans who are tricked to misuse faith through inaction or action that is lead by our own wisdom rather than God's. When we commit to pursuing safety in Abba and waiting for His direction, we are no longer susceptible to Satan's plan of using a questioning voice to cause us to doubt Abba. This is because, as Jesus said, we will know the voice of Abba, the peace of God, and the Word of God. Thus, the questions that arise from our insecurities and vulnerabilities will have no effect on our lives. We will have the full confidence to move only under the direction of our Father, whom we know without a shadow of a doubt is protecting us.

WE ARE SECURED

There is a level of security in our identity that comes from being aware of the battles that Abba fights for us. Our security needs, beliefs, and breaches in our identity reveal what we believe about God's investment and involvement in our lives as Abba, our protector. If a person can never resolve or get victory over the constant reminders that nobody has ever stood up for him, then he is going to treat the Lord with a degree of suspicion. The person will question if Abba will do what others have done. There are so many believers who have had very few experiences of anyone standing up for them. That keeps these individuals from having faith in Abba, in a protective Lord. However, Hebrews 11:6 says, "But without faith it is impossible to please him: for he that cometh to God must believe that he is, and that he is a rewarder of them that diligently seek him." So the level of protection and security we need to bring assurance to our identity and to establish us as Abba's children is going to require faith in God to understand Him as our protector. We need faith in Him to have a clear view of Him; we need faith in Abba to love Him.

The orphan heart produces and promotes battle anxiety. It does that by voraciously fighting every battle in life alone and without the help of the Lord. This allows the orphan's identity to be riddled with insecurities and vulnerabilities that produce fear, nervousness, and discomfort when faced with a battle. Anytime orphan hearts sense a battle, anxiety will form within their hearts because they feel they have to fight by themselves; they believe there is no one reliable to depend on. That is why we see people today using the phrases "It is me against the world," "I can do bad all by myself," and "It's me, myself, and I. I am by myself." These statements are all signs of someone whose identity has not been rooted in Abba as a protector. Anyone who has ever known what it is to have a relational scenery full of friends, coworkers, and family members but still live with an internal sense that there is no one to rely on has yet to fully receive his identity as one who is secured in Abba.

Those who often find themselves quitting during battles do so because they have not resolved their understanding of Abba as their protector. They quit because they feel as if they fight alone. Yet those who have rooted themselves in the identity of Abba understand that they are one with the Father. They are never alone because their lives are filled with Father, Son, and Holy Spirit. If you are on a team, and exhaustion comes, you can tap out, and somebody else can tap in. In that team you rely on the strength of someone else to get you to the victory. When we are orphans in our hearts and in our identity, we feel as if there is no one to tap in to help us, no one we can rely on for strength, so we stop altogether. Some others do not quit during battles but may live a life full of inconsistencies. There are still places in their hearts that they have not surrendered and believed in the revelation of Abba as a protector.

God is the only One who can give us security. When we embrace our identity as secured in Abba, then we will have all the peace we need. We will no longer live as if there is no one reliable to help us. When we embrace Abba's identity as our protective Father, we will have security as His sons and daughters. Whenever insecurities and vulnerabilities want to show up in our lives, we will quickly be able to present them to God and await His direction for our lives. Our identity as secured means we are steadfast in Abba's ability to save us from whatever situation may come our way. We can have confidence not in ourselves but in Abba's ability to protect us and care for us.

Our identity is one that is confident and secured in Abba's protection. We were born to make Abba our hope and our refuge. We were born to weather all the storms of life because we can tap our Father in whenever we need Him. Abba's children were made for more of His love, mercy, and protection. As Abba's sons and daughters we can trust and believe that whether we are winning or losing in a battle, Abba still loves us. We can recognize that the byproduct of a battle won is not just ethereal, invisible victory. It is perfected love. Therefore we are not alone or lonely because we were made for love. We were designed and fashioned after the perfected love of our Father. The more we cry out for Abba in worship and surrender to His love, the more secure we will be in our identity as protected and in the knowledge that no matter what comes our way, Abba's will shall be done in our lives.

7

OUR TRUSTWORTHY FATHER

Abba's Will Be Done

God is not a man, that he should lie; neither the son of man, that he should repent: hath he said, and shall he not do it? Or hath he spoken, and shall he not make it good?

∞∞∞ NUMBERS 23:19 ∞∞∞

THE BIBLE IS a book of promises. It is filled with promises made, promises fulfilled, and those yet to be fulfilled. The entirety of the Old Testament kicks off God's promises to the world. The whole journey—from Genesis through the other books of Moses, the chronicles of the kings, the writings, and the prophets—records God's promise of a Messiah. The Messiah was God's answer to generations of genocide, homicide, wrestling, toiling, and fetishes. Believing in God's promises is not always easy, as some of these Old Testament stories attest, but it always proves to be worth it.

There is no one who better understands the complexities of God's promises than Moses. In the Book of Exodus God appears in a burning bush to Moses and tells him to go tell Pharaoh, the most influential leader of the time, to release the people of Israel from slavery. God makes Moses a promise that God Himself will come and deliver the people from the Egyptians and bring them into a land "flowing with milk and honey" (Exod. 3:8). I imagine that Moses is partly stunned and in awe when he says, "OK. Who am I supposed to tell Pharaoh sent me with this message?" (Exod. 3:13, author's paraphrase). And from the burning bush comes God's famous response, "And God said unto Moses, I AM THAT I AM: and he said, Thus shalt thou say unto the children of Israel, I AM hath sent me unto you" (Exod. 3:14). Moses had to ask God this question because prior to this experience he did not know that there was a God who made promises. Moses was raised in an Egyptian household and most likely never heard the stories of Abraham, Isaac, and Jacob. So when God shows up to him, the first thing He does is introduce Himself: "Moreover he said, I am the God of thy father, the God of Abraham, the God of Isaac, and the God of Jacob. And Moses hid his face; for he was afraid to look upon God" (Exod. 3:6). After introducing Himself, God tasked Moses with introducing God to the enslaved people of Israel. God was starting a new record of Himself among the people as one who keeps His promises.

Amid dramatic signs, wonders, and sheer miracles, God empowered Moses to confront demonic powers, principalities, spiritual forces, and rulers on a national scale. At the end of the fight, just as God promised, Pharaoh let Israel go. (See Exodus 4–14.) Moses and the people of Israel learned a valuable lesson during that time: I Am is a God who does what He says He will do. Moses realized that the I Am speaks personally to His people. When He does speak, whatever He says is important, and whatever He says will occur just as promised. Moses could take God at His word because God is bound to His word. And because God is bound to His word, the word could never fail. God went on to speak even more promises in Exodus to the people of Israel. He spoke a series of promises that yielded principles for governing and organizing themselves as a nation. God spoke to the people about His standards for their code of conduct. He spoke concerning how they should live and what He would do in response to their obedience in following His instructions. God even spoke regarding details of their everyday lives, such as their dietary restrictions, family order, and interactions with their neighbors. (See Exodus 20–24.)

When God spoke in the Book of Exodus and throughout the rest of the Old Testament, it was always with a promise on the backdrop. God once made a promise that Moses reiterated: "And it shall come to pass, if thou shalt hearken diligently unto the voice of the LORD thy God, to observe and to do all his commandments which I command thee this day, that the LORD thy God will set thee on high above all nations of the earth" (Deut. 28:1). Those who listened to God's words and obeyed His instructions would be blessed forever, according to the promise. In accordance with this promise, Moses reminded the people that whenever God spoke, they should pay close attention, obey, and await the blessing of His promised word.

Promise Fulfilled

In the Garden of Eden after the fall of Adam and Eve into sin God spoke a promise: "And I will put enmity between you and the woman, and between your offspring and hers; he will crush your head, and you will strike his heel" (Gen. 3:15, NIV). God's promise was that despite Satan's seeming victory over Adam, Satan would ultimately lose. God promised that a child would be born to destroy the works of the devil even though Satan would try to kill Him. After that time in the garden God made hundreds of promises concerning this child. From Genesis to Malachi the Old Testament is filled with the promises of God concerning what the child would be called, His character, and His mission and ministry. Promises, including the one found in Genesis 49:10, said He would come from the tribe of Judah and would gather all nations into obedience to God over and against the disobedience that was introduced in the garden. First Samuel 2:35 recorded a promise that He would be a faithful priest. We learn in 1 Chronicles 17:12–13 that He would reign on David's throne forever. The prophet Isaiah said the Lord promised He would send the Spirit of God, He would provide salvation for the world, and He would be a sacrificial lamb in accordance with Exodus 12 (Isa. 44:3; 49:6; 53:7). This was a promise that the child would be a lamb without blemish presented after the Passover to save us from wrath. Daniel 9:24 recorded a promise that

He would be a light to the Gentiles and would "make an end of sins." It was also promised that He would be a cornerstone (Zech. 10:4). In the final book of the Old Testament, Malachi, it is promised that He would be the messenger of the new covenant (Mal. 3:1).

Over four hundred years after the last promise made in the Old Testament concerning the child to come, God delivered on His Word. John 1:14 confirms it for us: "And the Word was made flesh, and dwelt among us, (and we beheld his glory, the glory as of the only begotten of the Father,) full of grace and truth." Just as Moses revealed, God does what He says He will do! Before we even knew the name of the child in the Gospel of John, we knew that He was the Word. He was the literal manifestation of every promise concerning the Messiah that God made from Genesis to Malachi. He was the visual demonstration that indeed God is bound to His Word. Even though the people had to wait to see the manifestation of God's Word, it did not disappoint, nor did His Word fail. The people waited on God, and the Word was a blessing, just as God promised. As a matter of fact, the Word was even better than they had imagined because when God makes a promise, He puts everything behind it. So the Word of God manifested full of glory, grace, and truth, and He was called Jesus.

The remainder of the New Testament reveals how Jesus Christ is the Messiah. He is the Anointed One who was promised by God in the Old Testament. Christ is a fulfillment of everything that God is and a perfect example of how much God invests in fulfilling every promise to His people, no matter how long it takes. Jesus embodied the promises in Genesis that said He would come from the tribe of Judah and destroy Satan's works of disobedience and sin. Christ's ministry on earth was to heal the sick, give sight to the blind, and set the captives free, as God promised in Isaiah 61:1–3. Through Jesus's death and resurrection He became the perfect sacrificial Lamb who brought forth salvation to both the Jews and the Gentiles. Christ empowered His disciples to launch the church of which He is the cornerstone or foundation. He sent the Spirit of God to ensure the success of all His disciples as He ascended into heaven to reign on David's throne forever as the King of all kings and Lord of all lords. God started the whole saga of loving, healing, and restoring His people through Christ with a word.

Thankfully God still speaks today! His promise is that we who receive God in our hearts as Abba will inherit every word Christ declared. God committed to fulfilling for us the hundreds of promises Jesus spoke in the New Testament. These promises include the one found in John 3:16—that we would receive eternal life— and that our Father will reward us openly (Matt. 6:6, 18). He promised that we would bear much fruit, have abundant life, abide in Abba's love, be filled with the same full joy that He had, and live as His friends (Luke 8:15; John 10:10; 15). Christ also promised we would do even greater works than what He did in His time of ministry on the earth (John 14:12). Greater works include healing the sick, setting the captives free through the casting out of demons, and speaking with new tongues (Mark 16:15–18). Over and above these documented promises of Christ and through the spirit of prophecy God continues to speak His personal word of promise to you and me, our families, our cities, and the nations of the world.

"I Am Not Your Broken Promises"

The cry for the more of God—more of God's love and more of God's power—within the church in this hour lets me know that we do not see the fullness of Christ's promises in our lives. If God is bound by His Word, and He promised we would inherit every word Christ spoke on our behalf, then there must be some disconnect. There seems to be a disconnect between God's word and the manifestation of His promises in our lives. Since it has already been established that Abba's Word does not fail, then we must investigate what is hindering us from seeing the fulfillment of Christ's promises and Abba's Word in our lives. I believe that the disconnect we experience is because our culture is lacking in integrity, filled with broken promises, overflowing with disappointment, and existing within the limitations of time.

A lot of our lateral experiences with human beings inevitably affect how we receive Abba in our hearts. The broken promises we have experienced in our lives at the hands of our fathers, mothers, family members, teachers, former significant others, or friends can make it seem as if no one keeps his promises. The stories we hear of preachers falling into sexual sin, mishandling money, and protecting their own interests before those of the church even lend to this idea that integrity is nonexistent. Unfortunately the judgments and conclusions we place on others often become the limitations we project on Abba. Therefore the same way that we expect nothing from people's word, we expect nothing from God. We stop looking for the manifestation of Abba's Word in our lives. Take a look at any election cycle, broken marriages, dysfunctional families, the prison system, and the marginalized sections of our cities and nation, and it will be easy to see that promises are made every day and broken. We have become conditioned to expect that promises will be broken and that hoping for integrity in someone is unwise. This only results in our treating God's promises with contempt.

Disappointment and the delay of promises being fulfilled also play a factor in our not seeing the fulfillment of Christ's promises in our lives. The presence of disappointment and trauma in our lives, if not healed, creates a hopelessness within us that often keeps us from believing that anyone's word is true. Living anchored in disappointment breeds skepticism that frames our lives with the mentality of, "I'll believe it when I see it." The problem is that we often take this attitude with us into our times of prayer and apply it to God's promises for our lives. This approach to life keeps us from seeing the manifestations of God's Word because, as Hebrews 11:6 says, "without faith it is impossible to please him: for he that cometh to God must believe that he is, and that he is a rewarder of them that diligently seek him." Faith fuels the impossible in our lives. When we don't believe God for the manifestation of His promises until we see them, there is no faith. There is no expectation in our hearts to propel God's Word to actively manifest. Therefore the Word of God for our lives remains dormant or happens without our even taking notice because we never stood in expectation of it.

The timing of the manifestation of promises mixed with untrained prophetic voices that speak their own words as opposed to God's word have also left many people to wonder if God's promises are sometimes broken. However, God wants you to know that He is not your broken promises. He is Abba, a promise keeper. Numbers 23:19 says, "God is not a man, that he should lie; neither the son of man, that he should repent: hath he said, and shall he not do it? Or hath he spoken, and shall he not make it good?" When God speaks, we should pay close attention, obey, and await the promised blessing. God is His Word, and because of that He puts the full weight of every resource He has to bring His Word to pass on behalf of His people. The limitations of living in time do not negate the promises of God; they are eternal. When God spoke the last promise concerning Jesus, it took four hundred years for His promise to manifest. God spoke promises to people such as Abraham, Isaiah, Sarah, and Jacob, and they never saw the manifestation of the promises in their lifetimes. Yet God is committed to His Word, so the fact that time on the earth was over did not mean God's Word was done. God fulfilled the promises He made to them through the generations that came after them, and He continues to fulfill those promises even today. Abraham, Isaiah, Sarah, Jacob, and so many like them believed God's Word, and the exercise of their faith gives us access through Jesus Christ to see the manifestations of God's promises in our lives today.

Our experiences with a lack of integrity, broken promises, disappointments, and the limitations of chronological time should never be the basis of our not fully receiving the revelation of Abba's Word and promises in our lives. Instead, they should be an inspiration to help elevate our expectation and faith in Abba's ability to bring forth the manifestation of His Word. If we look at our lives, I guarantee we can match some of the worst seasons of life to a promise of God. When God's Word seems to not manifest, it can also be a sign of an assault on a promise. Satan wants to continue the propagation of the lie that God is not a god of His Word. So his strategy is to distract our focus from God, dismantle our hope, and destroy our faith in God with disappointments and broken promises.

That was the strategy Satan deployed in the Garden of Eden. The promise God made to Adam and Eve was that human beings would have dominion, rule, multiply, and fill the earth (Gen. 1:26, 28). The devil fought this promise with a lie that ushered fear, separation, disappointment, and a lack of integrity into the earth because he wants to rule the earth. Since God's Word cannot fail, the promise of humans having dominion, ruling, multiplying, and filling the earth could not fail. So God countered Satan's lie with a promise about Jesus centuries before He was born. God promised that Jesus's destiny was to crush the head of the devil and restore humans back to their rightful place of dominion, as God originally spoke. God's Word not only set up humanity for redemption, but it also exposed the lie that Satan still tries to use even today to cause people to lose hope in Abba's promises.

Satan wants people to believe that God is not who He says He is and that His Word concerning us is not true. God's declaration concerning Jesus in the Garden of Eden countered that lie of the devil. Without God's Word in the garden the lie of the devil concerning Abba's identity and our identity in God would have continued. Hence God had to step in. Wherever you see a lie at work in your life, whether it be a lack of integrity, brokenness, or disappointment, know that God is speaking a promise for you. There is only one thing more powerful than a lie, and it is a promise kept. When Satan releases lies against you, God always speaks a sure word of promise on your behalf.

A TRUSTWORTHY FATHER

Every word spoken from the mouth of God is a word that can be trusted. Whereas Satan is the father of lies, Abba is the Father of truth. God's truth is not just an idea, a wind of doctrine, a psychological or physical research study, or what makes Him feel good on any given day. God's truth is a person, and that person's name is Jesus Christ (John 14:6). Through Christ we can understand Abba's identity as a trustworthy Father. To say God is trustworthy means He is the perfect reflection of integrity. In today's culture we crave integrity because we have so many broken promises and so many individuals who say one thing and do another. However, God's integrity is rooted in something even deeper than His actions. Abba's integrity is rooted in His heart as a Father. The father heart of God is to love us as His children. It is to see us as a reflection of His Son. God's heart is to protect us. It is to cover us with His Word. Therefore when God speaks a promise over us, it is not just about doing the right thing. God's Word also comes from the right heart posture and motive. The promises God speaks on our behalf are balanced. They encompass God's love for us, our identity in Christ as Abba's children, and God's protection, all working together for our good.

The hypocrisy of the Pharisees was such an issue for Jesus because He was well rooted in Abba's integrity of heart, word, and deed. The Pharisees seemed to have the right words, but their hearts were far from the truth. Their hypocrisy took them in the complete opposite direction of Abba's integrity. This is why Jesus would call them a brood of vipers, snakes, whitewashed tombs, and hypocrites, and then condemn them to hell (Matt. 23:27, 33). Jesus wanted to show God's disdain for their lack of integrity and dishonesty. He wanted to compare Himself and the Pharisees. The Pharisees were legalists who were selective in their application of the Word of God, applying it to everyone but themselves. However Jesus was consistent in the application of God's Word because He understood that God's Word held promises that could be trusted. Abba is consistent and completely trustworthy in all matters. Through Jesus's commitment to living as the Word of God made flesh, we learn that Abba is trustworthy in His words and levelheaded in His thoughts. God's point of view is always morally and ethically correct while being well balanced with His identity as a lover, protector, and promise keeper for His children. The Father is trustworthy because He is not just speaking promises and declaring words for His benefit; He is trustworthy because He is consistently seeking to bring us into the truth of our full identity. He is consistently looking to love us, see us, protect us, and speak words that will manifest our true place in Him as His children.

God's integrity permeates every facet of who He is as Abba. He is moving in integrity when He loves us. Integrity is in every decision when He protects us. When Abba says He sees us in Christ, it is trustworthy. When

God speaks to our past, present, or future, it is consistently reliable. At all times God is trustworthy because He is consistent. Abba is the same yesterday, today, and forever (Heb. 13:8). God will not be trustworthy today but break a promise tomorrow. There is no wavering in God. James 1:17 says, "Every good gift and every perfect gift is from above, and cometh down from the Father of lights, with whom is no variableness, neither shadow of turning." This means Abba does not make a decision or give us the gift of a spoken promise and turn around and say, "Oh, I made a mistake." This is why Abba's words are trustworthy: integrity consistently flows out of His character as a loving Father. Before God speaks on our behalf, He has already considered all the possibilities, seen all the pitfalls, and considered all our choices, yet He still chooses to speak the best outcome for our lives. Abba's identity as trustworthy means that not one of His words is ever going to fail. Therefore we can trust Abba at His word.

It may seem difficult to have faith when you do not see a word manifesting in the time frame you set, but God will fulfill His promise. The people of Israel had many difficult days awaiting God's promise. One of those promises was for them to build a permanent dwelling place for God among the people. (See 2 Samuel 7.) Finally under King Solomon the people built a temple in Jerusalem. At the dedication of the temple Solomon reminded the people, "Blessed be the LORD, that hath given rest unto his people Israel, according to all that he promised: there hath not failed one word of all his good promise, which he promised by the hand of Moses his servant" (1 Kings 8:56). Despite the difficulties and time it took to see the temple God promised to manifest, Israel and King Solomon celebrated the integrity of God and His Word! Indeed, it failed not, and the temple was built, as He promised. We can rest in God's integrity. The Word of the Lord is good; it does not fail because it originates from the essence of Abba's identity as our Father. We can trust God and believe that Abba is committed to consistently manifesting His promise for our lives.

PURSUE OBEDIENCE

God is richly invested in His promises for our lives. Abba proves this to us with His flawless integrity that is reliable, honest, consistent, and trustworthy. As we seek the more of God in our lives, we must relate to His integrity with a radical sense of obedience. Obedience is the best way to relate to God's integrity because it demonstrates our trust in and love for God. John 14:15 says, "If ye love me, keep my commandments." God's integrity is so filled with love that the only way to relate to it is through obedience. Our obedience is an act of trust in Abba's integrity, trustworthiness, and love through our faith. On the other hand, when we do not move in obedience, it shows the Lord that we do not love Him. In Luke 6:46 the Bible says, "And why call ye me, Lord, Lord, and do not the things which I say?" God's trustworthy word comes with instructions. His instructions are a road map to seeing blessings unfold. Therefore in order to see the promises of God manifest in our lives, we must be obedient to every instruction.

God has given each one of us the power of free will. This means we have a choice when God gives us instructions to be obedient or to do whatever we would like to do. God honors our freedom. When we choose to be obedient to the instructions of God, we get to see the manifestation of God's promises in our lives. The amazing thing is that, because Abba is a promise keeper, our disobedience does not negate His promises. No, His promises are eternal. What our disobedience does do is cause us not to see the manifestations of the promises in our own lives. Since God's promises are eternal and do not fail, the conditions of the promises are simply revised when we disobey, and they are instead fulfilled in the next iteration or generation. Consider Moses. God promised Moses and the people of Israel that He was taking them into the Promised Land, but Moses did not see the manifestation of that promise because he was disobedient (Num. 20:11). In fact, most people who heard that promise of a new land for Israel did not see the manifestation of that promise because of their disobedience. The next generation and Moses's protégé, Joshua, were the ones who got to see the manifestation of God's promise to give the people their own nation. God's promises are eternal. They will be fulfilled. We can either choose to partner with God through obedience to see the manifestation of His promises in our lives and during the seasons in which God desires for them to manifest, or we can choose to be disobedient and not see the manifestations of His promises.

In His infinite grace Abba gives us instructions we can trust so we can inherit His promises. Every instruction God gives has a corresponding promise. When we follow the instructions of God, the reward of obedience is the manifestation of God's promises for our lives. God does not change, so think about how many promises we have missed because we refused to follow Abba's instructions. This is why disobedience, rebellion, and even hesitation to obey always work against our well-being. When we are slow to follow Abba's instructions or do the complete opposite of what He said, we are partnering with Satan and our flesh against God. The devil knows that the way to keep us from entering into God's promise is to use rebellion or disobedience. Hence He sends fear, laziness, lethargy, disappointment, depression, and other weapons of mass *distraction* to encourage us to disobey God. Despite Satan's plan Abba is so invested in His promises that He prepares us to handle them by teaching us. He instructs us and gives us opportunities to obey. When we allow Abba to bring instruction to us through the Holy Spirit and those to whom God directs us, it produces another level of obedience in us. As we obey more and more, we receive more and more of Abba's promises. We receive Jesus as the initial promise. After we receive Jesus in our hearts, we graduate to the promise of baptism in the Holy Spirit, then into the righteousness of God. If you think about it, even salvation is a graduation of promises, with the ultimate promotion being eternal life. Each step of the process requires that we trust God's Word and move in obedience to the instructions the Father releases to us.

Obedience to instruction that yields a promise is a pattern in Scripture. For example, John 4 records that Jesus instructed the woman that she could drink of His water. After this instruction, Jesus promised her that she would never thirst again if she followed this instruction. She believed in Jesus at that moment as He instructed, and she was so satisfied by His life-giving message that it overflowed to her whole community. (See John 4:1–42.) God's instructions are to help us understand that He is a trustworthy Father. Our faith in His integrity manifests His promises. When we disobey, rebel, or hesitate on an instruction, we miss Abba's promises. Abba puts a timeless continuum to His promises, which are only activated by the trust of His people. A promise cannot manifest on the bed of suspicion or the absence of trust. This is why we have instructions. The instructions help us learn Abba's identity as trustworthy. When God instructs us by His Word or counsel, He is preparing our lives to be suitable for the promises that are on the way. Abba is helping to boost our faith for the promises. When we operate in disobedience or hesitation, we have taken the bait of one of the most effective battle strategies of the devil. This strategy is to make people lose sight of the promises of God. It is a very effective strategy because when we are distracted, we do not follow up on God's instruction. Distractions keep us from valuing Abba's instructions. When we are distracted, we are tempted to not see the point of God's instruction. Therefore we will approach God's word of instruction casually, only on our own time and convenience.

The issue of disobedience, rebellion, and hesitation in submitting to God's instructions is the sin nature. The sin nature is not a sin act; it is what sin did to the human psyche. Humanity's sin nature creates certain beliefs about promises, the breaking of promises, the validity of promises, and the reliability of promises that determine and affect the depth of our obedience to God. If we are suspicious, cynical, or skeptical about a promise, it will affect our obedience. In other words, our level of obedience articulates what we really believe about a promise. Imagine how many people would be set free in their obedience walk if they did not have to struggle to believe God's promises. Visualize what our devotional lives would look like if we understood that all instruction from God is the seed of a promise from Him. Imagine if we believed that obedience waters the seed of instruction and brings forth a harvest of promises. We often get stuck in the instruction, but the promise is always bigger than the instruction. The instruction is the beginning of whatever God's promises are for our lives. So when we move in disobedience, we break the pattern of instruction and promise found in the Bible. This causes us to miss out on the far more superior promise and the knowledge that we can trust God.

Instructions are God's way of being a loving, protective Father. When we do not follow Abba's direction, we compromise His promises. We do so by trying to take our own action to bring about the promise. Abraham is an example of this; he had a child with a slave woman in an attempt to fulfill God's promise that He would be made into a great nation. Abraham's later obedience in sending Hagar and her son away did help him. He did not get to see the great nation, but Abraham did get an opportunity to see the seed start the process by the birth of his and his wife's son, Isaac. This is important because the promises of God are for us, but they may not always manifest in our lives. God's promises require our obedience because they may be seeds to begin the process of the promises manifesting even though we may not live to see the fullness of the promises. Therefore our obedience is vital because we have the opportunity to partner with Abba to see the promises of His purpose accomplished. Although the promises of God may have our personal lives as their focus, they also will have reverberating effects. When the baptism of the Holy Spirit came, Peter said, "For the promise is unto you, and to your children, and to all that are afar off, even as many as the Lord our God shall call" (Acts 2:39). The baptism of the Holy Spirit had reverberating effects throughout families and for generations to come, even to today. When we are obedient to Abba's instructions, we enter into this cycle of God's promises.

The promises of God manifest in cycles and dimensions. Our initial obedience causes God's Word to manifest at one level. In the cycle of God's promises they are only partially fulfilled when the manifestation of the Word of God only happens in one generation. Abba desires for us to see the promises of God manifest in our lifetime and through our obedience for generations to come to be blessed. God's Word is a promise with a legacy. This is what Abba gave us in Jesus Christ. Christ's obedience is our eternal promise that grants us a legacy of blessings. This is why obedience is so important: Jesus's obedience is further proof that obedience activates the promise of God for generations. It was the same for Abraham, Isaac, and Jacob. Abraham's obedience activated promises given to Isaac, Jacob, the nation of Israel, and to us today. That is why we Christian believers are called the seed of Abraham. We are a manifestation of a promise made to Abraham thousands of years ago that his descendants would be as numerous as the stars in the sky (Gen. 26:4). Even Jesus was born, generations later, through Abraham's obedience to God's instructions. Now, through Jesus's obedience, generations of people around the world can come into the knowledge of Abba, His identity, and their identity in Him.

What will generations say about your obedience?

Obedience is such a crucial step in receiving God's promise that Abba sent us some assistance through the Holy Spirit. Jesus said, "Howbeit when he, the Spirit of truth, is come, he will guide you into all truth: for he shall not speak of himself; but whatsoever he shall hear, that shall he speak: and he will shew you things to come" (John 16:13). In Scripture the Holy Spirit is called "the promise of the Father," a Comforter, a teacher, and "the Spirit of truth" (Acts 1:4; John 14:17, 26). Therefore in partnership with the Holy Spirit we have everything we need to receive every one of Abba's promises. It is the Holy Spirit who helps us walk in radical obedience. He also teaches us the different cycles and dimensions of God's promises. It is the Spirit of truth that leads us to embrace Abba's identity and our identity in Him. Abba gave us a gift in the Holy Spirit as an added measure to help us never miss a promise from God. When we partner with the Holy Spirit, we receive supernatural grace to obtain every promise in God.

AT REST

In your pursuit of obedience you will learn that every facet of your life and identity has a promise to it. There is not an angle of your existence that does not have a promise to it. The US Constitution teaches the only promises to life are life, liberty, and the pursuit of happiness. However, if you study Deuteronomy 28, there are promises from God about your body, destiny, finances, family, state of being, and even your real estate, or where you would live. These promises are components of your identity. Unfortunately most people never see all the promises of God richly fulfilled in their lives because they are not at rest in their identity as sons or daughters of Abba. If we obey the voice of God, we can be at rest in our identity as sons and daughters of Abba and experience His promises in our lives.

God's plan is for His Word to be fulfilled in us so we become an example of God's trustworthiness. This is obtainable when we partner with this by showing He is trustworthy by obeying Him and thus resting in our identity in Him. As Christ obeyed God and rested in His identity, He became the fulfillment of God's Word. Similarly as we obey God's instructions and rest in our identity as Abba's sons and daughters, and His promises are fulfilled in us, we become a living testimony to the fidelity of God. In Jesus, God's will for humanity was done. Abba intended that we would rest in the finished work of Christ on the cross and that through our obedience, in partnership with the Holy Spirit, we would serve as a testimony that God continues to fulfill His promises in the earth. Therefore our identity as sons and daughters of Abba is key to the manifestation of God's promises. Living fully in our identity as sons and daughters who are at rest in their identity begins with the revelation of Abba as our trustworthy Father. Our acceptance of Abba's identity leads us to pursue obedience to His

Word. In pursuit of Abba's Word, we find our own identity by resting in His promises.

Without the fulfillment of God's promises, people live unfulfilled lives; this is because when they do not see the promises of God, their hearts are broken. I often find that having a broken heart is directly related to a life that has never recovered from a broken promise. These broken promises can be a result of their doing or induced by someone else. Hearts are not broken when parents do not do as they should or because of a betrayal by friends; hearts are broken when something does not end up as expected, such as when a promise made in some way, either by implication or expectation, was broken. Brokenheartedness causes restlessness filled with anxiety, sorrow, grief, disappointment, and hopelessness. This is why God is the mender of the brokenhearted. How does He heal the brokenhearted? Abba heals broken hearts and fractured identities by giving a superior promise that far exceeds broken promises. This is what Abba did for Adam and Eve in the garden when their souls, bodies, and spirits were broken by sin. When their identity as God's children was lost and they embraced fear, anxiety, and the lies of Satan, God simply made a superior promise by promising Jesus Christ, who would come to restore and redeem humanity wholly back to the identity of sons and daughters. This ultimately causes us to trust and obey Him, which then allows us to rest in that identity and experience no more anxiety, sorrow, or hopelessness. We have the ability to embrace this restoration that God brings to our identity by resting in our identity as children of a trustworthy God, which we seek out by obeying Him.

Our deliverance from brokenheartedness and finding rest in our identity require us to pursue God's identity of being trustworthy through obeying. Abraham was willing to be obedient even though at that point in time humanity did not have as much documented evidence of God's faithfulness as we have today. However, Abraham decided to silence the fears, the doubts, the questions of "What if?" and "How is it possible?" to hope in God. In his pursuit of obedience Abraham was able to see the birth of his son Isaac, which ultimately fulfilled the promise of God to Abraham. Today in partnership with the Holy Spirit we can be at rest in our identity in God, and through that we can inherit every dimension of God's promises from long ago and become the person God uses to initiate His promises upon the earth to bless others for an eternity to come.

As we pursue obedience by placing our hope in God's promises, we not only find the revelation of Abba's identity trustworthy, but we also find our identity as sons and daughters called to rest in God. Resting in the promises of God aligns our hearts with our true identity as children of Abba called to rest in the Father's promises. Resting in the promises of God helps sustain us in times of stress and refocuses our vision. When we rest in the promises of God, we come into agreement with Abba that God's will shall be done in our lives and in the lives of others for generations to come. There is only one thing that will energize people in bad times, and that is the promises of God. Nothing else is as powerful as God's Word. Encouragement does not work. Friends are not powerful enough. Sometimes we do not even have it in us to keep praying for a promise.

As we rest in our identity as Abba's sons and daughters and await the promises of God for our lives, we can be confident that God will accomplish His promises. Let's place our hope in Abba's identity as our trustworthy Father and pursue obedience so we may find our rest as God's children who believe that Abba has the ability to empower, strengthen, and reinvigorate us to persevere until we see God's promise. We must live a life that pursues Abba's identity so that we can find our identity in His promises!

8

OUR INVOLVED FATHER

Abba's Rod

*Now no chastening for the present seemeth to
be joyous, but grievous: nevertheless afterward
it yieldeth the peaceable fruit of righteousness
unto them which are exercised thereby.*

∞∞∞ HEBREWS 12:11 ∞∞∞

GOD IS COMMITTED to seeing His sons and
daughters grow. He does not want us to stay
the way we were when we entered the kingdom of God.
When we received Jesus Christ into our hearts as our
Lord and Savior, we had just begun. It was our entrance
into the kingdom of God, but when you enter a home,
you do not just stand at the door. You move past the
door into the home, and the owner leads you as you go.
Growing in God occurs in the same manner. We enter

into the kingdom of God through Jesus Christ, and then the Holy Spirit leads us on a journey to grow into God's sons and daughters. I believe heaven and angels rejoice when we become saved because we sons and daughters have come home to grow into our identity in Abba. Heaven rejoices because God is invested in our growing.

Growing in the kingdom of God occurs through pruning. Jesus detailed the growing process:

> I am the true vine, and my Father is the husbandman. Every branch in me that beareth not fruit he taketh away: and every branch that beareth fruit, he purgeth it, that it may bring forth more fruit. Now ye are clean through the word which I have spoken unto you. Abide in me, and I in you. As the branch cannot bear fruit of itself, except it abide in the vine; no more can ye, except ye abide in me.
>
> —JOHN 15:1–4

Pruning is the removal of things in our lives that do not bear witness to the individuals our Father has called us to become in Him. The pruning process occurs through discipline. Sons and daughters of Abba must embrace all of Abba's identity as their Father. And one of the aspects of the Father's identity is that He disciplines and prunes us, His children. Abba's discipline and pruning is a demonstration of His love for us. The fact is God loves us so much that He will correct us instead of letting us go off in the wrong direction and get hurt, disappointed, or killed. Abba's discipline is always to be an act of His love to allow His sons and daughters to grow into the fullness of their identity.

CONDEMNATION

God's discipline is intended to be a display of His love for us. It even shows us that God's desire is for us to grow into the likeness of His Son, Jesus. Part of this growth is through the removal of those things in our lives that are not like Jesus. However, Satan has another plan: to make us believe that God's discipline is punishment. Satan brings condemnation and guilt upon us so we do not fully receive God's acts of discipline as displays of love, as Abba intends them to be.

Abba gave Moses various laws in the Old Testament, and these laws were intended to help the people of Israel live as a newly formed nation and as a people of God. The people of Israel were in the midst of an over four-hundred-year period of enslavement when God called Moses to go and tell Pharaoh to let God's people go. As God secured their victory from Egypt and led them into the wilderness, He gave Moses a set of laws to help in governing the people. The laws were intended to protect the people and help them live peaceably together with God and with one another as a nation. Among the laws were laws for conducting their affairs and the affairs of the nation and even for organizing their homes. The laws also included consequences for the people were they to fail to fulfill the commandments of the law. These consequences were meant to encourage the people to live in compliance with the law, and living in compliance with the law was important because it was a means of helping the people grow as a nation.

Over time the laws of God became closer to suggestions for the people rather than laws they were commanded to follow. Furthermore they were not growing into the nation God intended for them to become. Israel instead was growing to become more like the other nations around it. The people were chasing after the gods of those other nations and doing as they pleased or as they saw the people in other nations do. What was intended as good and an act of love for the people of Israel Satan used for his purpose; the laws became a place of condemnation and guilt. Instead of the people rejoicing that God cared enough for them to teach them to become a nation and instruct them, the people began to see God's commands as punishment. Condemnation and guilt became a way for the priest to control the people. This was never God's intention. He set forth the discipline of the laws as a way to foster relationship with His people, but they were never meant for punishment. They were meant for helping the people grow in their love for one another.

God's discipline was not wrong; it was good. The people enforcing the laws and commandants God gave were the ones who removed the identity of the Father from His laws. The discipline God designed for His people through the laws that were put forth in Israel continued to condemn the people until Jesus's arrival on the earth. Even then a religious sect in Israel used the laws to condemn Jesus to death. The religious leaders of the time took God's laws, which they did not fully understand, and used them against Jesus. When Jesus died, Satan must have thought he had won. Satan must have thought he had put forth the ultimate condemnation of the law by crucifying the Son of God. However, Abba had a plan of redemption. In Jesus Christ, Abba redeemed the law and fulfilled it. God's creation was no longer subjected to the condemnation of the law, sin, and death. In Jesus we can say, as Paul did, "There is therefore now no condemnation to them which are in Christ Jesus, who walk not after the flesh, but after the Spirit" (Rom. 8:1). Abba's sons and daughters are free to walk outside of the condemnation of the law and in the discipline of love from their heavenly Father.

"I AM NOT A PASSIVE GOD OR A DICTATOR"

There has been much debate and discussion concerning God's discipline and pruning. Many people do not properly understand it, so they either dismiss it as allegory or use it as a means of discounting and discrediting God. The first group of people, those who dismiss God's discipline and pruning, use 1 John 4:8 to defend their position: "He that loveth not knoweth not God; for God is love." They argue that because this verse says that God is love, then God does not discipline us. Many also claim that because Scripture says that God is love, then God does not have an opinion or a right to have an opinion on matters that are going on in our lives or in our society today. In their minds as long as we love what we are doing, then God is happy with us and the world. But arguing that God is love disqualifies the other aspects of Abba's identity, such as His justice, His holiness, and

His desire for His people to live by the standards that He outlined in the Bible. For those who argue God is love, the rest of the Bible could be thrown out, and it would not matter because they have chosen to focus on one aspect of God. For them a loving God means they can continue doing whatever they desire.

This statement, "God is love," is very true. He is our loving Father. However, that is not the only aspect of the Father's identity. He is as much a disciplinarian as He is love. He is as much a protector as He is a disciplinarian. He is as much a Father as He is a protector. God is Abba. He is not a God who is passive and aloof, nor does He desire for us to just go around doing things that make us happy and feel love. God is a Father; He is our Father. And as a Father His primary job is to make sure we grow into sons and daughters who are good, law-abiding citizens of the kingdom of God who hold the freedom to display His love, authority, and power throughout the earth. Abba is invested in our growing into sons and daughters. He is invested in our knowing and understanding our identity. He is invested in our embracing His love and identity.

There are others who acknowledge Abba's desire to discipline and prune them. However, they believe God's discipline is punishment and inhumane. They use this argument in an attempt to discount and discredit God. They argue that God is a dictator who forces people to do things His way and that when human beings do not comply, He orders for them to be killed. Oftentimes the individuals making this argument will use passages in the Old Testament, such as Deuteronomy 20:17, where the people of Israel were commanded to destroy the

Hittites, Amorites, Canaanites, Perizzites, Hivites, and Jebusites. They will use scriptures such as this as support for the idea that God sanctioned the murder of women and even children. They will argue that this form of discipline is inhumane punishment, and therefore any God who orders it is nothing more than a dictator who kills women and children.

But God is not a dictator. He is Abba, our Father. Those who seek to discredit and discount God always use only one aspect of God to try and build entire theologies about Him. However, God is not a one-line theology, nor is He defined solely by His actions. Abba is the sum total of God; He is more than the pieces and parts of His identity people choose to focus on. Abba's discipline for us today and His commandments recorded in the Old Testament and Deuteronomy to build a nation are motivated by the establishment of His love and laws for His creation.

Abba wants to be our Father because He loves us. When we receive Him as our Father, Abba presents to us standards in His laws that He invites us to live by for the rest of our lives through the power of the Holy Spirit. The establishment of His laws brings consequences. His integrity as a trustworthy God means He must exercise His love, His laws, and the consequences of these laws. If God did not uphold all these aspects of who He said He is, then we would have a right to say that He does not have integrity. However, Abba is completely trustworthy. Abba never forces us, as a dictator would, to do as He says. Abba grants each and every one of us free choice to make our own decisions at our will. Does He have a way that He desires we should go? Absolutely!

As a loving Father Abba is going to try everything in His power to point us in the right direction because He knows the other choices lead to destruction.

Abba does not want us simply to fall into destruction because we have no one leading us to the truth of God. Even though people want to use Abba's actions to paint Him as someone He is not—a dictator—God is still committed to making sure He provides for us, His children, the discipline, laws, and pruning we need to succeed and grow. Abba is committed to being involved in our lives and making sure He prunes us so we can grow into sons and daughters who love His instructions and plans for our lives.

AN INVOLVED FATHER

Every father can attempt to discipline his children, but only an involved father can do it well. When a father is absent in the life of a child and returns only to discipline the child, the father is usually met with resistance because he was not present to begin with. He has no history with the child, so there is no trust between them. The child will naturally see the father's attempt at discipline as authoritative and begin to question the father's motives. The same would be true for an abusive father. If an abusive father tries to discipline a child, the discipline will not be received well and may be feared. Fear never accomplished anything good, so disciplining a child through fear is not godly, nor is it the way God disciplines us as His sons and daughters. A child with an involved father can understand discipline in that he trusts his father to have his best interest in mind, even if he does not welcome the discipline.

Abba is an involved Father who disciplines us, His children, because He has our best interests in mind. Hebrews 12:5–7 reminds us: "And ye have forgotten the exhortation which speaketh unto you as unto children, My son, despise not thou the chastening of the Lord, nor faint when thou art rebuked of him: For whom the Lord loveth he chasteneth, and scourgeth every son whom he receiveth. If ye endure chastening, God dealeth with you as with sons; for what son is he whom the father chasteneth not?" When Abba disciplines us, it is a direct reflection of His recognition of us as His sons and daughters. A father does not have to discipline his children; many parents do not take the time or even feel their children are worth the time to correct them and lead them down the right path. Abba is not like those fathers; Abba's discipline is an investment in us that signals that He takes responsibility for us as sons and daughters (Heb. 12:5–6). The Lord does not take the time to invest in the lives of those whom He does not see as sons and daughters. But He takes the time for us, His sons and daughters. He takes the time to discipline us and make sure we are on the correct path in life because He wants to see us grow into the sons and daughters He always intended for us to become.

We can rejoice in God's discipline because Hebrews 12:6 says Abba disciplines us not only as an investment in our sonship but also because of His love for us. As an involved Father Abba's discipline is a direct reflection of His love for us. When a father is involved in the life of his children, he disciplines them when necessary to help them grow into the best possible human beings. When Abba disciplines us, His discipline is filled with justice, fairness, and duty. Through that discipline Abba teaches us how to treat others and ourselves with justice and fairness. We also learn the duty of sons and daughters. Each disciplinary act is tailor-made just for us to help us grow into the human beings we are being called to become. God is very intentional. He knows some of His sons and daughters can take certain forms of discipline, while others will only respond to another form. He knows when and how to prune and discipline us because He has been involved in our lives. He has been loving us and protecting us, so He knows the discipline that is most effective for us. His discipline has sympathy and care as well. Abba's pruning of our attitudes, motives, and thoughts is filled with grace as He teaches us what is right and wrong. This provides a sense of hopefulness even in the midst of discipline because it originates in God's love for us. We can trust in the hope of Abba's discipline because of the wisdom we gain through it to grow into the sons and daughters He has called us to become.

PURSUE WISDOM

We pursue Abba's desire for us to grow through discipline and pruning by pursuing wisdom. Wisdom is extremely important for us as Abba's children because it allows us to live out Abba's call of sonship for our lives. Without the wisdom of heaven we are without clarity and direction, and we lack understanding of where we should be going. When we realize that the Father desires to be involved in our lives, we must have a hunger and a thirst for His involvement and for the wisdom that it brings to our lives, even when that wisdom comes through discipline and pruning. The Scripture in Hebrews 12:11 is very honest: "Now no chastening for the present seemeth to be joyous, but grievous: nevertheless afterward it yieldeth the peaceable fruit of righteousness unto them which are exercised thereby." No discipline, even that from Abba, seems joyful. Discipline will grieve us at first, as if we are hurt, and we may mourn our old way of behaving. However, the growth that discipline produces and the wisdom we gain in the process will completely make it worth it in the end.

The Book of Hebrews says Abba chastens those He loves (Heb. 12:6); He chastens us by applying wisdom in an area of our lives in which we have been rebellious. He applies this wisdom to us through the power of His Word. That is why it is so important for us to take the time to read and study the Word of God every single day. When we are filled with the Word of God, then God can help direct us to the wisdom of the Word when He desires for us to grow in a particular area of our lives. Hebrews 4:12 reminds us, "For the word of God is quick, and powerful, and sharper than any twoedged sword, piercing even to the dividing asunder of soul and spirit, and of the joints and marrow, and is a discerner of the thoughts and intents of the heart." The Word of God has the power to discipline us and divide from us the thoughts and motives in our hearts that are not becoming of sons and daughters. The wisdom from the Word of God can keep us from becoming conceited or wandering astray or going down some other foolish path. When we are not filled with the Word of God, then our experiences and trials have a way of teaching us the wisdom of God and what He desires for our lives. The pain of mistakes can bring about wisdom when we learn from those experiences.

We can spare ourselves the heartache, experiences, consequences, and heartbreak of mistakes by pursuing the wisdom of God ourselves in His Word. We can pursue the wisdom of God by reading, studying, meditating on, and rehearsing the Word of God or through prophetic words and instructions from God spoken over our lives in our times of devotion or by others. When we are in the midst of making a decision or in need of direction, instead of making our own choices, which could lead to mistakes, we can pursue wisdom by always consulting God in prayer, by reading the Word of God to see what individuals in the Bible did in similar situations, or by reminding ourselves of God's instructions provided to use in the past. Abba's instructions are filled with wisdom for self-control, building faith, throwing off the things that hinder us, and more. The wisdom that God provides us through His instructions may make it seem as if He is disciplining us, but this does not always have to be the case. When we pursue God's wisdom, His instructions can also be a place of pruning us because God wants to reveal more of Himself to us. Consequently as He reveals more of Himself to us, we get the wisdom or understanding that develops more of our identity and character.

The more we pursue Abba's wisdom, both through the Word and through His discipline, the more involved He will be in our lives. We will find God willing to help us grow more into His sons and daughters and grow more in our understanding of the kingdom of God. Abba's discipline should be a priority in our lives as sons and daughters. In fact, we need to seek out and pursue Abba's discipline for our lives. Abba's wisdom and instruction should be a priority in every single area of our lives so we can become fruitful. We need to come into the revelation of Abba as our Father and pursue His wisdom in areas where we have been disobedient in the past. This should give us the confidence that Abba will chasten us and bring us into accountability to the principles of His Word.

WE ARE WELL BALANCED

Wisdom gives us an identity of being well balanced. When we pursue the wisdom and the discipline of Abba for our lives, we can be assured that our lives will be well balanced because we will be in sync with God's will. I meet people all the time who are searching for the will of God for their lives and people who are searching for their calling and purpose. My advice to them is to become a student of the Word of God by pursuing His wisdom, involvement, and discipline. The will of the Lord for our lives is in the Word of God. When we pursue the Word of God, we pursue the wisdom of God for our lives and we find the wisdom for our own identities. The will of God is the source of all wisdom and gives us the power to live well-balanced lives as Abba's sons and daughters.

It is easy to become so busy in life that we feel as if our lives are out of balance. We can feel as if there is too much on our plates. Particularly during those times we need to increase our pursuit of Abba's wisdom and involvement by reading and studying the Word of God. Often the opposite happens, and we begin to use our own earthly wisdom to help us accomplish our ever-growing task list. When we become overwhelmed, we tend to rely on ourselves. We are humans, and as such we will have a tendency to go back to what we know: trying to do it all ourselves! We will use our own strength to figure out what we should do in a situation, but when we do so, when we rely on our own earthly wisdom, life becomes a very lonely place for us. It begins to seem as if we have to figure out life of our own accord. In those moments we should simply remember that our identity as sons and daughters is to live a well-balanced life in Abba through pursuing His wisdom and therefore His involvement in our lives. Remembering our identity of being well balanced will inspire us to take the time we need to seek after Abba for His wisdom. Our pursuit of Abba's wisdom and involvement should be a daily pursuit. Every day we should seek to read the Word of God and commit to applying it to our lives.

In our pursuit of Abba's identity as our Father who is involved in our lives, we will find the wisdom to live a well-balanced life. Wisdom reprimands us and brings us back to balance through chastisement and discipline. As our lives become more in sync with God, we will realize that if we continue to keep our eyes and focus on God, then we will experience times of growth, even through discipline and pruning. Abba will grant us the wisdom to be balanced in our minds, bodies, and spirits. When Abba grants us balance in our lives, we have the stability and the steadiness we need. The stability comes from the wisdom of God, which we find as we pursue Abba's Word. We gain the balanced wisdom we need for whatever situation we face. We get a steadiness by knowing that Abba is our involved Father and that He loves us. Therefore whatever wisdom He is providing for us will be reasonable, sensible, and temperate with His love.

9

OUR CONSISTENT FATHER

Abba, Our Rock

*The L*ORD *is my rock, and my fortress, and my deliverer; my God, my strength, in whom I will trust; my buckler, and the horn of my salvation, and my high tower.*

∞∞∞ P*SALM* 18:2 ∞∞∞

T HE WORD *ROCK* is often used in a figurative sense to describe God. Moses was the first in Scripture to do so. Moses honors his experiences with God and tells the congregation of people before him, "He is the Rock, his work is perfect: for all his ways are judgment: a God of truth and without iniquity, just and right is he" (Deut. 32:4). During the wandering in the wilderness Moses got to experience the perfect works of the Lord, and during that time many of his experiences with God were centered around a rock. One example is Moses got to see God bring forth water from a rock (Num. 20:11). It was also in the wilderness that Moses was able to see the glory of the Lord. Moses found favor with the Lord, so He placed Moses in the cleft of the rock and allowed Moses to see His back as He passed by in full glory and splendor (Exod. 33:22). Through the wandering in the wilderness Moses came to know the consistent power of God to provide. God was the source of all of Moses's and the Israelites' blessings. They gained nothing not directly given to them by God's intervention on their behalf.

At the end of Moses's life he reflected on the miraculous events with Israel on the shores of the Jordan as the people prepared to enter Canaan and he prepared to die. Then Moses, for the first time recorded in Scripture, used the word *rock* to describe God, and in doing so he reminded the people that God was their rock and everything about Him is perfect. Moses equated a rock to strength and reminded the Israelites that it was God's strength that set them free from Egypt and the oppressive regime of Pharaoh. He reminded them that God was their source of strength in the wilderness. In the nighttime, when the people needed protection, it was God who manifested His glory as fire. Even though they sometimes traveled in the wilderness at night, God miraculously provided the light and warmth through fire that the Israelites needed to protect them. But during the day God was the pillar of cloud over the people to give them rest from the hot desert sun. God made sure to care and to provide for the people of Israel consistently. There was nothing the people needed that God did not provide them with. He simply wanted to be their God and for them to be His people. Abba was willing to go to great lengths for them to raise them up as a nation so nations all around would come to know Abba's love.

TRANSACTIONAL LIVING

As we just recapped, Moses took the time to reflect and remind the Israelites of the miraculous works of the Lord as he was preparing to leave them. Deuteronomy 28 provides a list of all the blessings God desired to grant the Israelites as a nation. The first fourteen verses of the chapter contain a list of all the blessings that were available for the people. God promised that He would protect them from their enemies. Moses promised them God's provisions and blessings upon their land. There are also blessings provided for their individual lives. Moses promised the people that these blessings are available through God, their rock. God was ready to provide for the people as they were in need when they moved into the Promised Land. The blessings were numerous, and these blessings were for the people as long as they remained faithful to the Lord. If they remained faithful, then they would always have provision and blessings of everything they needed in the Promised Land.

On the other hand, if the people were not faithful to the Lord, then there was an equally long list of curses they would experience. The first part of the chapter lists blessings they could experience, but the second half of the chapter provides a list of curses that would overtake the people of Israel for their disobedience. The curses would touch their individual lives. There are curses of sickness that would come upon the people if they disobeyed God and did not remain faithful to the Lord. There were curses upon the provisions of the people as well. The disobedience of the people would cause the weather patterns to change, Moses told them, and bring hardship upon their land. The nation itself would come under a curse if the people were disobedient. The Lord wanted a full commitment from the people to walk in total surrender to the Lord. He had fought for their release out of Egypt, He protected them in the wilderness, He was their Father, He was their strength, and He wanted to be respected for providing for them in their past as well as whatever they would face in the Promised Land.

The promises of God in Deuteronomy 28 turned out to be exactly as Moses described. When the people were faithful to the Lord, God showered them with blessings. They were victorious over their enemies, and they advanced into the Promised Land. The blessings of the Lord were with the nation of Israel even though they faced great enemies. In their faithfulness God was there, providing for them at every turn. He continued to move mightily and miraculously on behalf of people. When the people failed to be faithful to the Lord, they suffered great personal and national defeat. Their lack of faithfulness brought upon them much calamity. The inconsistency in the level of faithfulness in the people over time created a culture in which the people believed that God was a transactional God. The people thought that if they needed something from the Lord, they simply needed to posture as if they were faithful and God would show up with blessings for them. So they would try to be faithful to God, God would bless them, and then the people would return back to their same old ways of being unfaithful to God. Their unfaithfulness inevitably led to curses. Their transactional lifestyle led to a continuous cycle of blessings and curses.

On their own the people could not sustain the requirements of God to be and remain holy before the Lord at all times. They needed help, and God was willing to provide that help for His people. God sent His Son as provision into the world to provide for the many ways that the people missed the mark and could not live up to their end of the covenant to be faithful to God. Abba sent the perfect offering for the law through the life, ministry, and death of Jesus. Not only was Jesus the fulfillment of the prophecies; He was also the perfect fulfillment of the law. Jesus was able to perfectly fulfill the faithfulness of God, which was needed to manifest all the blessings of Deuteronomy 28. As a result of Christ's faithfulness each and every one of us who believes is able to live fully in the blessings of His grace. We no longer have to strive to become worthy of God's blessings. Christ's suffering for us made it possible for those of us who believe in Him to walk in the full blessings of the Lord and the full provision of God, our rock, at all times in our lives. We have the ability to see the perfect work of Abba, our rock, in our lives, in our families, and in our nations. In Christ we have the gift of seeing His truth and experiencing the just reward of Abba's righteousness in our lives.

"I AM NOT INCONSISTENT"

Transactional living did not start with Deuteronomy 28. The human race has always participated in some form of transactional engagement. Another example of transactional living is experiencing consequences and repercussions for our actions. The things we think, say, and do all have some type of consequences attached to them for ourselves or for others. Our actions are like throwing a stone in a pond; they cause ripples that spread out and affect things and people around us. We live interconnected lives, so the actions we take today rarely affect just us; they will affect many. Our lives are transactional in the sense that each day we complete a set of actions to get a certain agreed-upon thing in return. In other words, we go to work to get an agreed-upon salary. We pay an agreed-upon price for an item at the grocery store. Transactions are a big part of our lives. Some people will even approach church as transactional, even attending a certain church to gain a certain title or a status level for their family.

The issue with transactional living is that we project these limitations on God. We assume that being transactional is God's temperament. So many people live out their relationship with God using this model. They believe that if they attend church regularly, then God is obligated to bless them and make sure there are no hardships in their lives. They believe that if they pray the sinner's prayer, then they are home free and never have to do anything else. They think that because they attend church every Sunday, they are going to heaven and are good to go for the rest of their lives. But there are so many people with perfect church attendance who will never see heaven. They have a relationship with church but never really began a relationship with God through Christ. The issue with transactional living is the limitations it places on God. A relationship with Abba is so much more than just doing the bare minimum. Abba is

God, and He wants a relationship with us rather than checklists and to-do and not-to-do lists. This is why Abba was willing to invest His Son, Jesus Christ, in the earth. He was willing to send Jesus to live and die because Abba does not want legalism or mere checklist Christianity to limit our desire to become His sons and daughters.

God does not want to live merely a transactional relationship with us. Transactional living is inconsistent, and that is the complete opposite of Abba's identity. Moses validated this in Deuteronomy 32:4 with his declaration that God is a rock, because rocks are far from being inconsistent. Our actions do not exist solely in a vacuum; they touch and affect many other people. We can expect that when we initiate an action, there will be a reaction. However, the various actors in the scenario can do or act differently than we expect, which makes the outcome inconsistent. This is similar to the Israelites, who went back and forth between blessings and curses because of their transactional framework for life. However, when God gave Moses the words to share with the people of Israel in Deuteronomy 28, it was to paint a picture of the consistency, uniformity, and reliability of His identity. The inability of the people to control their actions and obey God's directives is what led to their thinking that God is transactional in His identity. Yet God demonstrated that this is not true by sending His Son, Jesus, to die for our sins. If God were transactional, Jesus's act of complete mercy and grace would only happen if humanity had done something to deserve it. Humanity could not have done anything to deserve God's grace and mercy through Christ because, as Romans 3:23 reminds us, "All have sinned, and come short of the glory of God." Abba's investment of Jesus was not because of a transaction or a law that was maintained correctly. Sin causes us to be inconsistent. God demonstrated that He is not transactional in His nature and character by sending Jesus, despite our inconsistencies, to die for our sins so we can be restored into our rightful place as Abba's sons and daughters.

Our conclusion that God is inconsistent is often drawn from our own expectations. We will expect that when something happens to us, God must react in a certain way, or we may expect God to do the same things for us that He did for someone else. Then, when we do not see God reacting in the way we expect, we think God is inconsistent. This is especially true when people say, "I think God is mad at me." People often say they believe God is mad at them because they did something they believe He does not like; because God does not like their action, they conclude that He is upset with them. "When I am good, God is happy with me, and when I am bad, God hates me" is a limitation that comes from the conclusion that God is inconsistent and transactional in His dealings with us. However, Abba is not inconsistent. As a Father Abba does not hate His children. He consistently loves them. As His children we may do something that disappoints Abba, but He does not hate us because we missed the mark. The Father is waiting to provide for us, waiting to help us, and waiting to redeem us. He loves us as His sons and daughters. We may need to be reprimanded, disciplined, or pruned to help us bring back balance in our lives, but Abba does not change how He feels about us. He moves in complete knowledge of who we are, and that doesn't change with our actions. If we handcuff God to behave a certain way, then we will miss out on seeing His miraculous moving within our lives.

A CONSISTENT FATHER

Moses could have used so many different things to describe God to the people. Moses and the people of Israel spent forty years in the wilderness together. During this time they got to see a lot of different things: trees, birds, and even the different mountains they had to climb to get from one location to another. There were many options Moses could have used when it was time to share with the people of Israel about God. As the people prepared to get ready to cross into the Promised Land, Moses began to recount for them God's identity. As part of the people's punishment for not wanting to go into the Promised Land earlier, everyone except Joshua and Caleb died in the wilderness over the forty years. Thus, when Moses was sharing about God's identity, many people present were of a completely different generation. They did not see the miraculous working of the Lord. It was up to Moses to share with them God's identity. This was a big moment, and Moses chose to tell the people that God is a rock. I think Moses chose a rock because he wanted them to get the imagery that Abba is consistent.

When we think of a rock, we think of something that is consistently the same. A rock is not a rock today and tomorrow a bird or a snake. In the same way that a rock is consistent, God is consistent. We can count on

Abba. He is reliable and dependable. No matter the situation or circumstance we can count on the Father to always be our heavenly Father. This can be a hard concept to understand about the Father because our world is filled with so many people who are unpredictable and who change with any weather, form, or doctrine. However, that is not the case for Abba. Abba says of Himself, "For I am the LORD, I change not; therefore ye sons of Jacob are not consumed" (Mal. 3:6). Our Father is consistent so that at any point in time we can always trust Him enough to come unto Him. Abba is consistent in His character toward us and in how He loves us. We can expect those things to never change. As a rock is consistent, so is God going to consistently be present in our lives. Even when we are inconsistent, God is consistent. Even when we are unreliable, God is reliable. No matter what changes in the world, there is one thing we can always count on: Abba. Abba always acts the same way toward us. He is loving and He is consistent regardless of our moods. He loves us just as much on our bad days as He does on our good days.

Abba's consistency means He is also filled with power and ready to exercise His power on our behalf. We don't always think of a rock having power, but a rock has a lot of power. If you throw a rock, it has the power to hurt someone or worse. David used a rock to kill Goliath (1 Sam. 17:49–50). Rocks also have the power to hold together whole buildings. They are often used in the foundations of buildings because they are solid and durable, which is needed for construction. In the same manner our consistent Father should be the foundation of our lives. His power provides support for us as we grow into strong sons and daughters. He is also available as our power source ready to destroy our enemies for us.

Abba is always faithful to us, His children. Abba is always present at all times to display His power on our behalf. God's power is dependable for us. Abba is consistently working on our behalf. This ensures that His power can be trusted. Abba is consistent as our rock in every circumstance and with the power to give us victory in every situation we may face in life.

PURSUE SURRENDER

Abba is consistent in all His dealings with us. He is reliable, stable, and dependable. We relate to Abba's identity as our consistent Father by pursuing total and complete surrender to God. When we surrender to God, we lay down all of our inconsistences from our sin nature by committing to follow Abba's lead. We accomplish this by receiving God's identity as a consistent Father and letting that become our identity by being uniform in our attitudes and stable in our actions, just as Abba is. Moses realized God's consistent love and power; Exodus 33:15 says, "And he said unto him, If thy presence go not with me, carry us not up hence." Moses refused to do anything without God. Abba's consistency requires that we refuse to do anything, to pursue anything, or to think of anything without Abba's voice, Word, and presence. We must totally surrender to His leading. When we talk about Abba's identity as a rock, we are talking about something that cannot be moved. And although His actions vary, His views about us remain unchanging, and we can be confident to surrender to His leading and to follow Him on both our best and our worst days. When we pursue complete surrender to Abba, His consistency, or the dependability and reliability of God with His promises, grants us the courage to accomplish any task before us and gives us the security we need to be victorious. We pursue complete surrender by praying, denying ourselves, and relying on God.

Praying

Surrendering to Abba, our consistent Father, is a daily pursuit that starts in our prayers. When Jesus taught His disciples the model prayer for communicating with God, He included "Thy kingdom come, Thy will be done in earth, as it is in heaven" (Matt. 6:10). Our prayers are a key to surrendering our inconsistencies to Abba's consistent nature because they provide us with the instructions and assurances from God that we need to accomplish His will. As we pursue surrendering to God, our prayers should be for Abba's will to prevail in our lives and around the world. The more we surrender to Abba's identity as a consistent Father, the more consistent we will become in our prayers and our lives. The Father's identity will become our identity when we surrender to Him.

Denying ourselves

When we surrender to God, He reveals even more of Himself to us. We can surrender to Abba's consistency by denying ourselves; we deny ourselves by uniformly choosing Abba's will every opportunity we have. To deny ourselves means that we say no to what we desire and say yes to what God desires of us. When we come to believe that God is stable and dependable, then we become willing to forgo the things that we have placed our hope in, such as money, a career, or prestige—things that become idols in our hearts. We exchange the idols of our pasts for the promises from God in our future. We accomplish this by denying ourselves through spiritual practices such as fasting, self-control, and submission. The process of denial is the process of humbly yielding ourselves and our desires to the Lord. Denying ourselves is a very hard task to do. Even Jesus had to live a life of complete and total surrender to the Lord. When Jesus was in the garden of Gethsemane, He had to make a decision to choose His will or to choose the will of God. Jesus chose God's will by denying Himself. Jesus said, "Father, if thou be willing, remove this cup from me: nevertheless not my will, but thine, be done" (Luke 22:42). Jesus had to pray and ask God to help Him deny His own will so He could choose instead to do God's will. Jesus's full surrender was hard because it led Him to the cross, but it was completely worth it because His pursuit of surrendering to God allows every one of us who believes in Jesus to become Abba's son or daughter. As we pursue surrendering to God, we will also experience moments when it may become difficult to consistently remain in pursuit of Abba. Jesus's life and ministry teach us that, in those moments when our desires may lead us to attitudes and thoughts inconsistent with Abba's identity, we can draw closer to God by communicating with Him or by reading, studying, and meditating on the Word of God. The Word of God gives us the confidence, strength, and inspiration we need to help us accomplish God's will. It also helps us see that since

Abba is consistent, we can give up the inconsistent ways native to our sin nature and surrender to Abba's identity.

Relying on God

When we are surrendered to God, then we rely on God to work things out. We do not rely on ourselves to solve things. We seek our consistent Abba at all turns and in all circumstances. When we are aware of our Father's consistency, we will find it easier to surrender to Him by denying ourselves and praying for the strength of God to help us. A surrendered child of Abba is no longer susceptible to transactional living. The more we surrender, the less we carry the weight of the world on our shoulders. Surrendering ourselves, our will, and our thoughts to God is not a sign of weakness; it is living in the wisdom of God. By surrendering to God, we are empowered to succeed in what Abba has called us to accomplish as His sons and daughters. Surrendering to God does not always make sense to us, but it will always be the best way for us to receive both the peace and the freedom God brings in His consistency.

WE ARE UNMOVED

Abba's consistency helps shape our identity as Abba's sons and daughters. The use of the rock metaphor reminds us of Abba's identity as a consistent Father who is stable, dependable, and reliable. As our rock Abba is consistent in His character to love and protect us. He consistently provides strength to us. He is consistently solid and strong as our God. As we pursue surrendering to His consistent identity, His identity of consistency lends to our identity.

In the midst of surrendering to God, our identity as sons and daughters who are unmoved is revealed. If our Father is consistent at all times, then we are called to be steadfast in our identity in Abba and unaffected by whatever events may come against us in life. We are unmoved by circumstances, unmoved by situations, and unmoved by whatever life may bring because we are firmly anchored in our Father God, who is our rock.

When we embrace our identity as Abba's sons and daughters, we are unmoved because our faith is surrendered to the consistency of our heavenly Father. During our lifetime we will face various events that will encourage us to lack consistency in our relationship with Abba. During difficult situations our tendency may be to waver and to be inconsistent in our pursuit of surrendering to God through prayer, self-denial, and relying on God. But God does not waver in His consistency toward us, so we must be steadfast in our relationship with the Father. Surrendering to God allows us to remain unmoved, to remain faithful to the Father. We remain faithful by focusing not on our circumstances but on Abba's consistency as our Father. We focus on His ability to stand throughout times and circumstances and on God's ability to endure hardship. When we focus on God's consistency as a Father who is dependable and reliable, we are able to gain the strength we need to endure any circumstances we face in life. When we focus on our Father's power in all situations, we are able to gain wisdom and insight into the power He provides to us as His sons and daughters to overcome the situations we face at any given moment of our lives.

The goal for us as sons and daughters of Abba is to surrender to God so we can live in the fullness of our identity as unmoved sons and daughters of God and so we can become people who are resolute, decided, and unswayed despite the circumstances, situations, and doctrines presented. We do not allow people, things, and even words contrary to what is written in Scripture to change our attitudes, our understanding, or our beliefs toward God. Through surrender we become unmoved. Our revelation as sons and daughters is to recognize that the highest authority in the created world is whatever comes out of Abba's mouth. Through surrendering to His direction, guidance, and leading at all times and for all situations, we will be unmoved by what is happening in and around us. When we surrender to Abba by seeking after Him, God can grant us the peace, power, and assurance we need to not focus on our circumstances. When we go before Abba, then we have the explicit responsibility to materialize and obey whatever Abba says we are to do because in it we will find victory. In His leading we will find all that we need to transform our situations and our circumstances from hopelessness to hope and from defeat to victory.

When we are intently determined to believe in Abba as our Father and that His loving presence is consistently with us, then we can have the faith that no matter what Abba is working everything out for our good. Paul wrote, "And we know that all things work together for good to them that love God, to them who are the called according to his purpose" (Rom. 8:28). When we truly believe the revelation of Abba's identity as consistent in His love for and presence with us, then we are unmoved when difficulties arise in our lives. We are unmoved because we have faith in Abba that He is going to work out every event in our lives for our good. We have faith that no matter what Abba is reliable and dependable; thus He will come through for us and will change our circumstance for good. This is because the good that Abba brings is His ultimate good. Our surrender to Abba and His ultimate good helps us live fully in our identity as Abba's children who are unmoved because no matter what event we are faced with, we know that Abba's motives are always uniform, reliable, and constant. Abba is always looking out for the good of His children. Therefore we can daily pursue surrendering our inconsistency to Abba by trusting that Abba is our rock, our consistent Father. We are empowered to live completely in our identity as Abba's children who are unmoved because we are submitted to God's identity as our consistent Father. We can consistently have faith knowing that God will work for our good, even if the good is not exactly how we envision it. Despite the events of our lives we can be assured that God will always fulfill His identity as Abba Father, who loves us, sees us, protects us, rescues us, delivers us, and sets us on the path of victory as His sons and daughters.

10

OUR GOOD FATHER

Inheritance

*A good man leaveth an inheritance to
his children's children: and the wealth
of the sinner is laid up for the just.*

∞∞∞ **PROVERBS 13:22** ∞∞∞

As believers in Jesus Christ and as children of Abba all of us are richer than we could ever imagine. We are rich because of our inheritance. An inheritance is when a family's fortune is passed down to the children. The Bible has many stories of people giving, receiving, and fighting for their inheritance. From these accounts we learn that an inheritance was considered a gift or a special honor that fathers would pass down to their children in order to provide for and support them. The inheritance was not only for provision; it was also provided by the patriarch to make sure that the status of the family continued on the earth long after he was gone. A father who did not provide anything for his children was either poor or considered wicked for not caring enough to provide for his family. Abba, our heavenly Father, saw to it that we, His sons and daughters, would never be without an inheritance upon the earth. In the Old Testament Abba's inheritance for the people was land for their nation, which He promised to Abraham (Gen. 13:15). God gave Israel the Promised Land, which was a gift to help provide for and support them. The land that Abba gave to them was flowing with milk and honey, which means the land provided abundantly in agriculture and other resources to ensure their needs were met (Deut. 31:20).

As if the inheritance of the earth were not enough, Abba increased the inheritance for His sons and daughters by making it more lavish and extravagant. In the New Testament, through Jesus we were also given a spiritual inheritance (Eph. 1:11–14). Therefore we are far wealthier than we realize because we have an inheritance in Abba. Paul put it this way: "Wherefore thou art no more a servant, but a son; and if a son, then an heir of God through Christ" (Gal. 4:7). This means that we who are members of God's family through Jesus, Abba's sons and daughters, have a share in our Father's riches, including treasures such as the riches of His glory, His grace, kindness, patience, wisdom, and power. (See Ephesians 3:16; Romans 2:4; 9:23; 11:33.) Every inheritance that we have in Abba is invaluable.

Our inheritance, like God's promises, has multiple dimensions. For example, we receive the spiritual inheritance of salvation when we become believers in Jesus Christ. When we receive the baptism of the Holy Spirit, we receive spiritual inheritances such as boldness, and we are given the ability to speak and pray in tongues and are empowered with the ability to bear fruit consistent with the Holy Spirit. When we die, we will receive the spiritual inheritance of heaven. All of these dimensions of our inheritance are accessible to us because of the death and resurrection of Jesus Christ.

Christ's death made God's spiritual inheritance for us active right now! For example, at Jesus's resurrection all power and authority was given to Him, and as joint heirs with Him we have access to that power and authority instantly (Matt. 18:18–19).

Jesus said, "Verily, verily, I say unto you, He that believeth on me, the works that I do shall he do also; and greater works than these shall he do; because I go unto my Father" (John 14:12). When we walk in our identity as Abba's sons and daughters, we have the power and authority to accomplish even more than Jesus did on the earth. And when our time on the earth comes to an end, "We have a priceless inheritance—an inheritance that is kept in heaven for you, pure and undefiled, beyond the reach of change and decay" (1 Pet. 1:4, NLT). At the appropriate time in our lives we will receive the fullness of our spiritual inheritance through Jesus Christ as we stand face-to-face with our Abba in heaven. Until then we are given limitless and vast access to change the world to the glory of God.

THE INHERITANCE OF GOD

The inheritance of God is an incredible gift, but it was a gift that humanity at one time lost. When Adam and Eve through their sin chose to separate from Father God, they became orphans. Whereas Abba had provided protection, provision, and identity for them, once they were orphans, it was up to them to create their own identity, toil for their own provision, and fend for their own protection. They lost their home, as Genesis reads: "Therefore the LORD God sent him forth from the garden of Eden, to till the ground from whence he was taken. So he drove out the man; and he placed at the east of the garden of Eden Cherubims, and a flaming sword which turned every way, to keep the way of the tree of life" (Gen. 3:23–24). Adam and Eve were driven from their place of residence in the garden to the wilderness of the earth, and with this they lost their spaces, place, and futures. They were still God's creation, but they lost their name and identity as God's children. They were in bondage to labor, desires, and emotions, and they lost their authority as rulers with dominion upon the earth. Ultimately they lost the future Abba had for them and the inheritance they would have had as God's children. So because there was no inheritance, they had nothing to pass down to future generations except the sum of their choices and decisions. This is the inheritance that Adam and Eve left for all the individuals, including you and me, who would be born on the earth. We were born having lost our place of residence in heaven. We were alienated from our name as children of God. We were rejected from God and our future purpose. We became fearful of how

God and others saw us. We became isolated from our space and inheritance in the kingdom of God.

Our story could have ended there. However, God sent His Son, Jesus, to the earth to help restore humanity back to their inheritance in Him. In Christ's death the debt for sin was paid and the consequences of sin and death were removed so we could have the power and authority to live in our purpose and inheritance. Everything that plagued Adam and Eve in the Garden of Eden was reversed. Jesus descended into hell and with all authority and power took back the keys to our identity. Though the legacy that Adam and Eve passed down was death and a lack of identity, the legacy changed with Jesus. As I mentioned several chapters ago, if all Jesus did was pay the debt for our sin and reclaim our identity from hell, this would be powerful. But Jesus went further than that. He was resurrected from the dead! Through His resurrection, God's hope for us to come into our inheritance can be fulfilled. Abba finds joy in receiving us as sons and daughters so that we can access our spiritual inheritance of treasure, including the riches of His glory, authority, grace, kindness, patience, wisdom, and power!

God's plan to bring all who believe in Jesus back home to the kingdom of God and to their inheritance as sons and daughters through the death and resurrection of Jesus Christ was successful. As sons and daughters we are now free to enjoy rulership, dominion, and relationship with the Father, which is our inheritance. We are free to spend time in the presence of the Father. We are free to bask in the love of the Father and free to never have to leave the Father, but to live inseparably. We are free to see what He sees and trust that we are tucked safely under His arm of protection. We are free to experience His mercy and His involvement in our lives to assist us in living a well-balanced life. We are free to rest in His consistent love and to do His will on the earth as the manifestation of His promises. Abba's invitation is to freely be in relationship with God and to fully live in our inheritance as sons and daughters every single day of our lives.

"I AM NOT WICKED"

Jesus gives us access to a spiritual inheritance of sonship with Abba that is filled with power and authority. When we do not fully live in our inheritance as sons and daughters of Abba, we live as orphans, as they typically do not have an inheritance. Proverbs 13:22 says a good man leaves an inheritance for His children. So when we do not live the fullness of our inheritance, it is as if we are making a statement that God's proposed inheritance is not good. Our choice to live as orphans is an indictment about God the Father and about what we believe concerning Abba's identity. The orphan heart is without any direction because it has no inheritance to draw from as the source of its identity, nor does it believe there is a legacy it is called to create in response to its inheritance. Orphan hearts cause us to have a spirit of independence and desire for control, which affects our relationship with Father God and skews our vision of God.

Those with orphan hearts believe they have no inheritance because orphan hearts are always on the outside looking in at what is going on in the home. Those with orphan hearts feel like outsiders. They feel they are outside of the heart of the Father, as if they are fatherless. Orphan hearts feel as if they are outside of everything that belongs to the sons and daughters. Thus orphans do not believe the plan of victory that Jesus won for sons and daughters belongs to them. They do not believe that the freedom Jesus secured through His death and resurrection belongs to them. In addition, the affirmation and honor that sons and daughters receive from having their Father's inheritance is a foreign concept for those with an orphan heart.

The classic example of this is the story of the prodigal son, found in Luke 15:11–32. This story is familiar to most of us. It is a story about two different sons. The first son demanded one day what was due to him from his father and left. We are not told what happened between the two to cause the son to see the father as such a wicked person that he had to leave; we are just told he asked for his portion of the family's money and he left. This first son chose to live as an orphan. As a result of rebellion and pride he rejected his father's upbringing and went off to a faraway land, where he led a wild life. He had placed an indictment on the father when he left, as if the father was wicked. He clearly had a skewed view of the father. His inability to see his father's true identity left him broken and with an orphan heart. During this time the second son, the older of the two boys, stayed home and worked hard, but he also lived with a skewed view of the father. Even though he was home with the father, he still had an orphan heart. He still saw himself outside of the home and outside of the inheritance of the father. This son made the same judgments concerning the father that the first son made. When the younger son returned and their father rejoiced, the older son was upset and angry with the father for being so gracious and welcoming the younger son because he already had made a decision about the father's identity. He judged that the father was wicked for being so nice to the son who left. He was also judging that he himself must not be valuable because the father had never thrown him a party. Each son saw his father as a bad or wicked father. However, the father in this story is a great representation of God our Father. The father in this story teaches us that God is a good Father! He is a good Father who has an eternal inheritance for us as sons and daughters. He desires that no matter where we are, we receive His inheritance for our lives. If we choose to leave Him, Abba is such a good Father that He is still standing with open arms, waiting for us so He can love us, clothe us, and celebrate us as sons and daughters, just as the father did for the first son. He is also such a good Father that for those of us who have been believers of Jesus Christ for a long time but have found ourselves outside and with orphan hearts, He is also standing with open arms, ready to receive us, love us, clothe us, and celebrate us as sons and daughters, as the father desired to do for the second son.

The parable of the prodigal son is a reality for so many people today who have made a judgment against God. It is a reality for unbelievers who judged God based on their assumptions as well as believers of Jesus Christ who have not embraced the revelation of their spiritual inheritance as Abba's children. Like the two sons in the story unbelievers and believers not living fully in their identity as Abba's sons and daughters are all living with orphan hearts. The orphan heart has created definitions, limitations, expectations, judgments, and conclusions about God that distort His identity and seek to make God out to seem bad, wicked, unpleasant, or somehow morally incorrect. However, God is not wicked, evil, or lacking in His identity as Father. Abba is actually a good Father. He is thoughtful, morally upstanding, and suitable for whatever our lives may bring. God's goodness is bound to us as His sons and daughters. Not only is God good in His thoughts, actions, and promises toward us, but He also gives care and concern for our futures by preparing an inheritance for us. God has a name, a place, and an inheritance set aside for each one of His sons and daughters. Look around. The things we see on the earth are merely signs and wonders of the even greater and more extravagant spiritual inheritance God has for us. He has names set aside for us as His children. He adopts us and brings us into His own home. And Abba gives us names that are far superior to anything else we could have been called; he gives each of us the name of son or daughter. Then He gives us a home within the kingdom of God as an inheritance.

When we are not living in the fullness of our inheritance, we are lacking in our vision. We project our judgments upon God, and they can be used to draw negative conclusions about Him. However, God is not bad or wicked. Abba is a good Father. He is worthy of our love, trust, and commitment to living lives that glorify Him. God is not a bad Father who leaves nothing for His children. Abba is a good Father who is consistently providing for and supporting us now and for eternity.

A GOOD FATHER

As I stated, Abba is not a bad or wicked Father who leaves nothing for his children. He is a good Father who takes the time to prepare an inheritance for us. As a good Father Abba prepared an inheritance for us in Jesus Christ before we even realized His identity. He prepared for us a spiritual inheritance that we would receive on the earth and live out for eternity. Abba was so hopeful that we would come to know who He is as our good Father that He prepared for us, planned for us, and waited for us to walk into the knowledge of His goodness. His goodness toward us is manifested in doing good for us, providing for us, supplying for our temporal wants, and exercising His mercy to us. Abba is consistently there to provide what we need, to protect us, and to grow us as strong sons and daughters. Not only does He provide for our physical needs with things such as shelter, food, and clothing, but He also provides for our spiritual needs with things such as patience, love, skills, and abilities. Abba exercises His goodness by showing mercy toward us. Mercy is withholding punishment for what we deserve. Even though Abba allows consequences when we make wrong choices, He is always looking to show us His loving-kindness and goodness. After all, Scripture says, "And we know that all things work together for good to them that love God, to them who are the called according to his purpose" (Rom. 8:28). Abba is a good Father who is always present to support us with His goodness and to cause everything in our lives to work out for good. He is a good Father, so no matter what our circumstances may bring, what we would choose to do at any particular time, or what particular needs may arise in our lives, He is present and available to bring goodness for us.

Abba's goodness watches and waits for us until we turn to Him. As in the story of the prodigal son Abba's heart is good toward us, His sons and daughters. Abba's response to us as His children is not a mean "I told you so" after we realize our wrongdoing. Our Father is good; He does not wait for us to come into His identity so He can declare we should have known better. He is not waiting to ridicule us or make us feel as if we have no inheritance, place, or name. As a good Father Abba is waiting for us in eager expectation of our arrival into His kingdom. Abba desires for us to come into an understanding of Him as our Father. In the story of the prodigal son the father was waiting with expectation for the son. The Bible says, "But when he was yet a great way off, his father saw him, and had compassion, and ran, and fell on his neck, and kissed him" (Luke 15:20). The father was waiting to celebrate the return of the son. Abba waits with the same expectant heart to celebrate us. No matter what situations we find ourselves in, we can be confident that our heavenly Father is always waiting for us. He is waiting to declare His abundant, enduring goodness upon us. We do not have to live with orphan hearts. We are free to live from the vantage point of sons and daughters of Abba, the good Father, who loves and is attentive to us.

God is a good, gracious, and loving Father. As a good Father God wants to spend today, tomorrow, and eternity with us. He is not absent, distant, occupied with other things, uninterested, or broken in His view of Himself and us. No! Abba is secure in His identity as a good Father and confident in our potential to be good sons and daughters. He is not too tired or too busy, and He does not lose His way. God, our good Father, works at all times for our greatest good. Our Father loves us enough to teach us hard lessons and wants our lives to be meaningful even though it may not always be easy. As a good Father, Abba shows us that we are important to Him by dreaming big dreams for our lives. He sees us as His precious children, beautiful and worthy, just as we are, yet worth enough to not let us stay as we are. Abba's love for us is much bigger than our momentary comfort; it is developing and raising us to be like Jesus. Abba went through extraordinary lengths in Jesus Christ's death and resurrection to bring us home to Him. He wants to be with us now and forever, and He will do anything to make that happen. He wants a relationship with us. He wants our hearts to respond to His goodness and desire above all to become sons and daughters with hearts for their Father.

PURSUE GOODNESS

Abba is a good Father; He creates an inheritance for us and wants nothing more than to be our perfect Father, to heal our every wound, and to bring us into the fullness of what He intends for us to be. We relate to Abba's identity as a good Father by pursuing His goodness. We pursue God's goodness by answering our call and by building to the glory of God.

Answer the call

All believers have a ministry call regardless of where they are employed. No matter if you are in business, education, the sciences, media, government, or ministry, or are a stay-at-home parent, God has a call upon your life. You can pursue God's goodness by answering that call. This call for us is first and foremost to be sons and daughters of Abba. We answer this call not only by receiving faith in Jesus Christ as our Lord and Savior but also by believing in God's identity as our Father, Abba. We are called to believe in the full revelation of Abba's identity as a loving, liberating, inseparable, merciful, protective, trustworthy, involved, consistent, and good Father. In our pursuit of Abba's goodness we answer the call to believe in the full revelation of Abba's identity, and we then can come into the revelation of more of our own identity. We pursue God's goodness by consistently keeping the revelation of our Father's identity before us and sharing it with others. When our gaze is focused on Abba, then we have the ability to answer the call to be sons and daughters of Abba who share our revelation of Abba's identity. It is easy because our focus is not on things such as accolades, titles, money, or social status; instead, our focus will be on bringing all the glory to Abba.

Our pursuit of Abba's goodness encourages us to answer our call by following Jesus's example in John 5:19, when Jesus said He did as He saw Abba do. We follow the example by pursuing goodness by focusing on what Abba sees and doing what He is doing. Pursuing goodness by answering the call means our hearts' desire will be to multiply Abba's identity, perspectives, and actions on the earth. If we pursue His goodness, our hearts are always ready to say yes to Him and to our call! This is true no matter what industry, relationship, service, or action God has personally called us to accomplish for the kingdom of God. Our pursuit of Abba's goodness is not independent of our work, relationships, or actions. As a matter of fact, our pursuit of His goodness will always lead us to point others to our good Father in our actions and point to His desire to welcome all people home into His kingdom as His sons and daughters.

Build

Our pursuit of God's goodness is in recognition of our good Father's desire for us to be His sons and daughters. As we pursue His goodness, it leads us first to answer the call, and then we move into action by sharing the news about our Father with others to build the kingdom of God. We build the kingdom by making disciples of Jesus Christ. After Jesus's resurrection He took the eleven remaining disciples to the top of the mountain in Galilee and told them, "Go ye therefore, and teach all nations, baptizing them in the name of the Father, and of the Son, and of the Holy Ghost: Teaching them to observe all things whatsoever I have commanded you: and, lo, I am with you always, even unto the end of the world. Amen" (Matt. 28:19–20). Making disciples for the kingdom of God is the key to pursuing God's goodness.

Pursuing the goodness of God encourages us to build for the kingdom of God because of the joy we get to receive when other sons and daughters come back home to their rightful place in Abba. Not only do we celebrate, but heaven celebrates as well. Luke 15:10 tells us, "In the same way, I tell you, there is rejoicing in the presence of the angels of God over one sinner who repents" (NIV). Part of building is not stopping after rejoicing over the return of a son or daughter to Abba's kingdom. Our pursuit of Abba's goodness is also a call to provide the training and equipping needed to see to it that sons and daughters become mature sons and daughters in the same way that Abba provides training and equipping for us through His discipline and pruning. This is what the Great Commission Jesus shared with the disciples (quoted above—Matt. 28:19–20) reveals to us about our identity. Jesus could have simply celebrated His victory over sin and death and then taken His seat at the right hand of God the Father. However, He chose not to just remain at that mountaintop experience. Because of His love for Abba and recognition of Abba's goodness, Jesus came back to His disciples and countless others to give them the instructions for doing as He did. The Gospel of Mark lists Jesus's instructions this way:

> And he said unto them, Go ye into all the world, and preach the gospel to every creature. He that believeth and is baptized shall be saved; but he that believeth not shall be damned. And these signs shall follow them that believe; in my name shall they cast out devils; they shall speak with new tongues; they shall take up serpents; and if they drink any deadly thing, it shall not hurt them; they shall lay hands on the sick, and they shall recover.
>
> —MARK 16:15–18

When we receive the revelation of Abba as our good Father and we pursue His goodness, we do so by doing things our Father did through Jesus Christ. We go into the world, share about the goodness of our Father, and help others come into agreement with the revelation of Abba's identity and their identity in Him. We do not just stop there. We accompany people on their journey to becoming mature sons and daughters by casting out demons, teaching them how to not become ensnared by the snakes or temptations of Satan, and teaching them to drink the cup of suffering and still remain victorious. We also help them mature as sons and daughters in Abba by laying on hands and praying the prayer of faith in Jesus Christ that heals the sick areas of their lives. When we pursue goodness, we are empowered with the ability to build for the kingdom of God in such a manner because Abba is a good Father. We have the power and authority in the name of Jesus as Abba's sons and daughters to build the kingdom of God everywhere we go—at church, in our industries, in our relationships, within our communities and nation, and in nations around the world.

Refusing to pursue the goodness of God by building lends to the crisis we are seeing on the earth today. If we do not answer God's calling to fully open our hearts to the revelation of His identity as Abba and to point others to that revelation, then we will continue to see the current crises of immigration, globalization, nationalism, humanism, and fear of the future driving an identity crisis within our world. This identity crisis is manifesting not only in the current state of our national governments and economies but also in the church. The state of the world continues to be as it is and revival continues to tarry because so many people do not know and have not been told that they are not orphans who have to figure out life on their own—but that they are sons and daughters of God. They have not been told that there is more to life. They have not heard that their identity is in Abba. Not pursuing the goodness of God by answering God's call and building the kingdom to the glory of God is literally a life-or-death issue for someone each of us knows right now. It is critical that we embrace Abba's identity and our identity in Him because we have the power to change the world to the glory of God.

WE ARE SONS AND DAUGHTERS

In our pursuit of Abba's goodness, as shown to us through our inheritance, we find our identity simply as His sons and daughters. This is God's vision all along for our lives, that each one of us would become His son or His daughter. To be sons and daughters is to fully receive the revelation of the Father's identity as we fully embrace our own identity. This is how we receive the more of God that we have been singing for, praying for, and desiring in our lives. This is how we solve the identity crisis in our world. This is how we see revival on the earth.

These things happen when we walk in the fullness of our identity as sons and daughters by leaving a legacy. We pursue Abba's goodness by answering our call and building the kingdom as sons and daughters of Abba, and it results in our leaving legacy. Legacies come from the past and speak of those who left them behind for us. Typically parents will leave legacies for their children. Our ancestors left legacies for us and for our families.

After we leave this world, the legacies we leave behind will speak of our lives. These legacies can be positive or negative. We can have positive places of inheritance in our bloodlines, such as abilities, skills, or gifts, and we can also have negative inheritances in our bloodlines, such as curses of fear and anxiety. Similarly we all have legacies, and they can speak to the effects we are having on other individuals while we are alive. Even a baby who dies in infancy has some effect on the family he or she was born into. Something will change on the earth with the existence of each human life. When we embrace Abba's identity as a good Father and choose to fully live in our identity as His sons and daughters, we end up doing good things on the earth that leave legacies of the Father's goodness upon the earth. Each of Abba's sons and daughters should leave such a legacy. In fact, we should be concerned with it because when we do embrace our identity as sons and daughters by pursuing Abba's goodness, the legacies we leave declare that our Father is so good that He is worth sharing with generations to come. That's a legacy we should all strive to leave.

By pursuing Abba's goodness and fully living in our identity as Abba's children, we build our legacies each day, whether we are aware of it or not. The legacies we leave should come from our pursuit of Abba's goodness because the goodness of God is our rightful inheritance as sons and daughters. The goodness of God is the outrageous, lavish, unexpected, and undeserved kindness of Abba, as shown by our inheritance found in Christ. It is made available for us, and God wants us to make it available to others as well. He is good, and our identity is to be His sons and daughters who work good on the earth for His glory and to share His identity with others.

As we seek to live fully in our identity as Abba's sons and daughters, we must stay focused on Abba's identity. We must stay focused on His identity as a loving, liberating, inseparable, merciful, protective, trustworthy, involved, consistent, and good Father because it is the framework for how we are to live in our own identity. The pursuit of Abba's goodness delivers us from distress and breaks the chains of sin that seek to bind us or skew our identity. There is no superior source of deliverance for our identity issues than staying focused on Abba's identity. When we stay focused on Abba's identity through our pursuit of His goodness, our own identity as Abba's sons and daughters is strengthened; when our identity is being strengthened, we are reminded of the call to build a legacy to the glory of Abba. As Abba's sons and daughters we must remember that we are to pursue the goodness of God because Abba is the original definition of good. He is good in and of Himself. For us Abba's goodness is our identity. The goodness of God comes naturally for Him as a good Father. When we live fully in our identity as sons and daughters, then goodness will become natural for us as well. Just as Abba is constantly working for the highest moral and excellent good on our behalf as His sons and daughters, we will always look to do the same. He does this by showing His extraordinary goodness to us and to everything concerning us. Abba's goodness is extravagantly bountiful; He causes fruit to come from our lives. Abba does not just fill us with goodness and then leave us. He fills us with His goodness so we can go and share that goodness with others.

Through Jesus Christ you and I have access to an amazing legacy and inheritance. We have access to the more of God. We have access to the more of God as we embrace His identity as our Abba. The legacy we inherit in God is priceless. Our inheritance is the ability to become Abba's sons and daughters. As Abba's sons and daughters our inheritance includes His love, freedom, mercy, protection, trust, consistency, goodness, and Holy Spirit living within us. We inherit, as His children, the same power and authority that Jesus has, which awakens us to our identity and our call to be multipliers of the kingdom of God. As we pursue the goodness of God and live completely in our identity as Abba's sons and daughters, we do as our Father does. We leave a legacy as well—not just for our families, but for generations to come—to the glory of God.

NOTES

CHAPTER 2
OUR LOVING FATHER

1. "Matthew Henry's Commentary," Bible Gateway, accessed May 31, 2017, https://www.biblegateway.com/resources/matthew-henry/Matt.3.13-Matt.3.17.

CHAPTER 4
OUR INSEPARABLE FATHER

1. *Strong's Concordance*, s.v. "Shachah," http://www.biblestudytools.com/lexicons/hebrew/kjv/shachah.html.

2. William Temple, *Readings in St. John's Gospel: First and Second Series* (London: Macmillan & Co. Ltd., 1963), 67.

CHAPTER 6
OUR PROTECTIVE FATHER

1. *Strong's Concordance*, s.v. "yeshuwah," https://www.blueletterbible.org/lang/lexicon/lexicon.cfm?Strongs=H3444&t=KJV.

2. *Webster's Revised Unabridged Dictionary*, s.v. "buckler," http://biblehub.com/topical/b/buckler.htm.

ABOUT THE AUTHOR

MATTHEW L. STEVENSON III is the senior pastor at All Nations Worship Assembly in Chicago and the overseer of The GATE Network, which has churches all over the world. He enjoys pastoring his church, teaching, traveling, writing, and spending quality time with his children, both natural and spiritual. Stevenson has three children (two daughters and one son): Naila, Micah, and Karis. He has been married to his amazing wife, Dr. Kamilah Stevenson, for thirteen years. When it comes to writing, Matthew Stevenson likes to write on topics that are going to bring people into a deeper revelation of God and help bring His viewpoints to the attention of man. Prior to full-time ministry, he was a highly matriculated academic working for the public education sector, both as a practitioner and in public administration. Stevenson hopes to continue to travel the world as his career in ministry progresses. To date he has visited seventeen countries to minister, and that number is steadily rising. This book is only one of eight he has published, and there are many more to come soon.

CONNECT WITH US!

CHARISMA HOUSE

(Spiritual Growth)

Facebook.com/CharismaHouse

@CharismaHouse

Instagram.com/CharismaHouse

SILOAM

(Health)

Pinterest.com/CharismaHouse

MODERN
ENGLISH
VERSION

(Bible)

www.mevbible.com